slow

‹LONDON›

ROBIN BARTON & HAYLEY CULL

PHOTOGRAPHY BY
MARK CHILVERS

Affirm press

hardie grant books
MELBOURNE · LONDON

This edition published in 2010 by

Affirm Press
1 Jacksons Road Mulgrave
Vic 3170 Australia
www.affirmpress.com.au

Hardie Grant Books
85 High Street Prahran
Vic 3181 Australia
www.hardiegrant.com.au

National Library of Australia Cataloguing-in-Publication entry

Barton, Robin
Cull, Hayley
Slow London
ISBN: 978-0-9803746-9-8
Slow Guides; 4.
Includes index.
London (England)-Guidebooks. London (England)-Description and travel.
914.21

Designed by D'Fine Creative in conjunction with Sense Design and Stephen Walker
Printed in China by C&C Offset Printing Co., Ltd.

Disclaimer
All reasonable steps were taken – allowing for bad days, personal dramas, distractions and frequent lie-downs – to ensure that all the information in this book is accurate and up to date. Apologies if we've missed anything.

People to thank
Luke Redmond, Mike and Gavvandra Higgins, Caroline, Carl Honoré, Tom Hodgkinson, everyone at Slow Food London, Beth Hall, the Mayo kids, the Keogh-Burnett kids, Jonathan Thompson, Ed Bartlett and the countless people who shared their ideas, insights and love of London along the way.

The Authors

Robin Barton is a London-based journalist who contributes to several newspapers and magazines, including the *Independent on Sunday* and the *Evening Standard*. He lives south of the river but roams far and wide on his bike looking for things to write about, which may include food, sport, travel, architecture or even foraging for mushrooms on Hampstead Heath. As the author and editor of numerous travel guides to far-flung destinations, he's always glad to come home to witness London's gradual transformation into a city that can do the good life as well as the fast-paced, time-is-money stuff.

Hayley Cull helped devise the Slow Guides series with her contribution to the original title, Melbourne. This southern bird migrated north soon after, and has been looking at London through a slow lens ever since. When she's not flitting about the city she writes a bit, gets distracted a lot and spends far too much time in bookshops. She co-wrote and edited this book from under her favourite apple tree in south London, an idyllic little spot that's probably to blame for any wistful wittering within.

The Photographer

Mark Chilvers specialises in portrait, travel and feature photography, and has been extensively published in more magazines and newspapers than is worth mentioning. His career has taken him on many adventures, although not many quite as slow and satisfying as this one and he believes that with creative vision you can see more in a walk round the block than others might in a trip round the world. He is also involved in community teaching programmes in south London as well as completing his Masters in documentary and photojournalism.

About this Book

Slow London is co-published by Affirm Press and Hardie Grant, two publishers committed to publishing books that 'influence by delight'. It is part of a series that began with guides to Melbourne and Sydney, and is being published alongside Dublin.

This book was created with the combined efforts, ideas and energy of about a dozen people (plus all those we spoke to during our 18 months of research – you didn't expect us to rush it, did you?). Co-publisher Martin Hughes created the series, and used his editorial wisdom to bring this whole book together, with help from Beth Hall and Rebecca Starford, who also proofed the lot. Lara Morcombe created the rather spiffy index.

The look for the series was designed by Sense Design, refined by Stephen Walker, and further tweaked by Elena Petropoulos and D'fine Creative who put together this book. Gemma Viselli produced the illustrations.

Local

Natural

Traditional

SENSORY

Characteristic

A Slow Start

Sitting in my local park as the sun slides behind a ragged old oak tree, it's hard to believe I'm at the heart of the most frenetic and densely populated region of Europe. Dogs are being walked, couples bask in the light and sounds of laughter and splashing spill from the lido. The rattling trains and constant traffic dissolve into the background and I put aside my book to savour the moment.

'Slow' and 'London' are two words you don't often see together but this book – a manual for those who have daydreamed about downshifting to Dorset but couldn't bear to leave their friends, their jobs and city behind – aims to change that. The roots of the Slow movement, first Slow Food then Citta Slow, are in Italy but its branches have reached fact that Britons work the longest hours in Europe, with one in six Londoners working a 48-hour week, shouldn't be a source of bravado but concern (we address this issue in the Work chapter). But the economic shocks of 2008 and 2009 prompted many of us to look again at our lifestyles and ask, what exactly are we doing on this treadmill?

As we struggle to cram more into each day, we lose sight of what life should be about and lose touch with the world around us. It's no coincidence that stress, anxiety and depression are on the rise, with surveys showing more people are taking time off due to stress than ever before.

In recent years there has been a dawning realisation that some of life's simplest plea-

The word 'slow' is used 65

worldwide over the last 20 years. The slow ethos is about celebrating and supporting everything local, sensory and natural. Not just food but people, places, traditions and experiences. It's about appreciating all the little things that enrich our lives, which tend to be sidelined by the hurly-burly of the city. It's about doing something better, not faster.

Modern life tantalises with the promise of immediate gratification; consumers are bombarded with messages that say we can have it all and pay it off later. This means keeping our noses to the grindstone. The sures are its most delightful. Slow has become a big deal in London: there are more cyclists on the road, restaurants state where their ingredients are sourced and knitters are spotted on the Tube. We'd like to take the concept of slow beyond Borough Market (although we'll definitely pause there for a roast pork bun with crackling); we won't lecture or hector but instead champion the local, the independent and the handmade – the Monmouth Coffee Companies of London rather than the ubiquitous international chains.

The first half of this book introduces the sights, sounds and smells of the city around us, its great buildings and green spaces. We meet London's wildlife and some of the experts who look after it. Culturally, we put a slow slant on the capital's museums, galleries and events.

Following that is Do, a practical guide to the capital, where we visit markets and libraries and the best city farms for children. We explore the city by boat and bicycle and then hop on a train for weekends away.

Slow is different for everybody; for some it will be in the crackle and pop of a vinyl record rather than the digital perfection of a download, for others it will be in cooking a meal from scratch with the family. It's about rediscovering your own equilibrium in a world gone crazy. Importantly, slow should not be a luxury for the privileged but an entire rethinking of our relationship with time

shortage of sunshine for half the year and crowded public transport – the city has an inexhaustible resource: its people. From urban beekeepers to guerrilla gardeners via a myriad of passionate individuals and organisations, London is kept vital by its citizens. So long as they're here, propagating exciting and unlikely ideas, London will be a fantastic place to live.

Indeed, this book is a collaborative effort. Local photographer Mark Chilvers brought a visual *joie de vivre* to the party, his black-and-white images evoking the mood of the city, the grey light we're so familiar with, and a sense that everything old is new again. Slow heroes such as Carl Honoré, author of *In Praise of Slow,* and Tom Hodgkinson, editor of *The Idler,* shared their time and insights very generously. We've asked Buddhist monks, entrepreneurs and naturalists, among others, for their take on living in London and

times throughout this book

in London. Neither is it about turning the clock back 50 years; technology has brought unthinkable possibilities to our lives and we won't resist its shortcuts. Rather, slow is about regaining control of our lives and putting the brakes on this runaway train. Becoming more mindful of how we live will benefit not just our health but also our communities, our environment and even our wallets.

At times this book was a challenge to write. Even with the most positive outlook, London can be an exasperating place. But despite its frequent frustrations – mine include a

all helped us get a little closer to our goal: reconnecting with London in as sustainable and pleasurable a way as possible.

So, taking to heart the Chinese proverb, 'A book is a garden carried in the pocket', we hope Slow London will arouse your senses, fire your enthusiasm and be as inspirational as it is practical. After all, even in a city of eight million people, it's possible to slow down and smell the roses. 🐎

Robin Barton

CHARACTER

WHAT SHAPES LONDON AND LONDONERS

TIME

NATURE

WORK

time

AGAINST THE CLOCK

> ## BE HAPPY WHILE YOU ARE LIVING,
> ## FOR YOU'RE A LONG TIME DEAD.
> Brendan Behan

Let's start at the end. Next time you pass a cemetery, spare a thought for the poor souls inside. Consider that they probably lived their lives pre-occupied with similar concerns that fill our heads today, and compare the weight of their worries with the lightness of their presence on the planet. If they could have a few more hours, do you reckon they'd spend them rushing from one meeting to another? Running an amber light so they could get to the gym before it closed? Or checking their email every 20 minutes? Probably not.

Isn't it ironic, though, that after all the effort we took to *capture* universal time, we ended up becoming enslaved by it? Hundreds of clocks in laboratories around the world now keep time accurate to one second within three millennia. They make it virtually impossible for time to slip away from us again; or for us to slip away from time. But perhaps those souls in the cemetery would think that the best timekeeper is not the clock but the heart, which measures not the passing of time but the *quality* of time we spend. If it's empty, perhaps we need to take, share and lose track of a little more time.

CANARY WHARF, 9:23AM

Out of Time

Although we get materially wealthier (apart from the recent 'blip') and technologically more advanced, it feels like we have an ever-dwindling supply of time. Days aren't getting shorter but we're increasingly hard-pressed to find moments for rest and recreation. Technology promised us more time for leisure, but instead strapped us to gadgets that constantly remind us of the time and the fact that we don't have enough of it.

City life is controlled by mechanical time, people by a biological clock. These competing clocks cause tension, irritability and a lack of focus. Tuning into the natural world helps 'clear our heads'. It may be as simple as a walk in the park, and we're blessed with patches of green knitted between grey streets.

Time looms large in London. The iconic Big Ben rises above the city, counting out our days, hours and minutes. Clocks stand sentinel all around us, on train platforms, on buildings. We have absorbed Benjamin Franklin's idea that 'time is money' but surely it's far more precious.

Perhaps we should focus on 'savouring' rather than 'spending' time.

Time After Time

Like a wrinkled old veteran – surviving plague, fire, the rise and fall of an empire – London's face tells many stories. There are lines of prosperity and hardship, science and faith, conflict and peace; character in every crevice. Noticing these layers reveals much about who we are.

PREHISTORIC LONDON

Walk down Old Bond St and, in between the glittering displays in the jewellers' windows, look closely at the limestone blocks used for the buildings. Those wisps and whorls in the stone are fossils; oysters, worms and snails, the earliest inklings of life on this spot. The Portland Roach limestone buildings are grand time capsules, hewn from prehistoric seabeds around the city.

Britain was once connected to the continent and as the seas rose animals were marooned on this island. Centuries later, giant fossils began to be unearthed: a mammoth in King's Cross, a three-metre long auroch (ancestor of the domestic cow) in Knightsbridge, a woolly rhinoceros under Battersea Power Station. Today the only evidence of these Ice Age fossils is in the Natural History Museum. The Victorians were so fascinated by their discoveries that scientist Robert Owens constructed a Dinosaur Court in Crystal Palace, where the life-size, if anatomically inaccurate, iguanadons and megalosaurs prowl the lake area today.

ROMAN LONDON

According to Peter Ackroyd in *London: The Biography*, if you stand at the junction where Gracechurch St divides Lombard St and Fenchurch St, you'd face the site of Londinium's Roman forum. The Barbican centre stands on the site of a Roman Fort and the Guildhall on an old amphitheatre. Remnants of the London Wall, built to keep out vengeful Celtic warriors, can still be seen in the walls of churches and buildings, and also behind Tower Hill Tube station. The Roman Empire may have collapsed, but its influence lives on today, in the spaces mapped out for the city's future.

The Romans got their first taste of the wrath of a wronged woman this side of the Channel from Boadicea, queen of the Iceni tribe of East Anglia. Marching on London with a 100,000 strong army in 60AD, she lit fires that burned so fiercely they left a geological layer of clay and debris that's still buried deep beneath parts of the city. Legend has it that Boadicea herself is buried under platform 10 of King's Cross railway station (but a thorough search of the area revealed only a secret entrance to nearby platform 9¾).

TUDOR LONDON

Medieval London was a maze of reeking alleyways, rife with disease and under constant threat of catching alight. And yet, under Tudor rule, this became a golden age for the city. Shakespeare graced the literary scene with his Globe theatre on the South Bank, and the open-air playhouse brought heckling, whooping entertainment to the city.

Church spires reached heavenward and Westminster Palace (now the Houses of Parliament) became a royal residence.

London's most sought-after residences – Westminster Palace, Lambeth Palace, Somerset House – were built on the Thames, the fastest and safest way to travel through the city. So important was the river that Henry VIII made it illegal to 'annoy the Stream of the River of Thames…by mining, digging, casting of dung, rubbish or other thing in the River'. The lusty old monarch may have had a green streak after all.

Fire struck in 1666, after the Tudor era, and London was redrawn in the most dramatic way. The Great Fire, which started in a bakery on, yes, Pudding Lane, destroyed about 13,000 houses, 87 churches and St Paul's Cathedral. The fire sparked a blaze of renewal. Once again, ambitious London, hungry to be bigger and better, pushed the fast-forward button, with buildings like Christopher Wren's sublime St Stephen Walbrook church and St Dunstan in the West, on which is mounted the first London clock to have minutes marked on the face. Few buildings in central London survived the fire, but luck graced the Seven Stars pub in Carey St. Over 400 years old, it still serves a consoling pint.

EMPIRE'S CAPITAL

'The deep hum of work-a-day London is upon us,' wrote journalist Blanchard Jerrold in 1868, 'and the church bells are musical through it, singing the hour to the impatient money-makers.' Trade from new colonies propelled London to become Europe's financial and commercial capital – you can still get a whiff of 17th and 18th century affluence with a wander through Knightsbridge, Kensington or Chelsea today. Time itself was calibrated at the Royal Observatory (see p22), and you only have to straddle the Greenwich Meridian to grasp London's influence in that sphere.

Euston, our first railway station, opened in 1837, its arrivals hall modelled on Greek temples. The world's first underground railway line, the Metropolitan Line, was ready in 1863. London's industrial past and its future come together in St Pancras: the Victorian Gothic station, designed by William Barlow and nicknamed the 'cathedral of the railways', is now the terminal for Eurostar with an ultra-modern new terminus designed by Sir Norman Foster. London as we know it today was really taking shape.

The Industrial Revolution was at its zenith, loudly proclaimed by Big Ben. But nature still fought back for the slowcoaches: London's iconic clock was slowed by four minutes in 1949 when a flock of starlings perched on its minute hand, and heavy snowfall meant the year 1962 started more than 10 minutes late.

POST-WAR LONDON

During the Blitz, Big Ben was untouched by bombs. But, in all other respects, time ran out for the British Empire. After the war Britain was broke. Many of the allotments we cultivate today were created during this time and simple pleasures were a necessity.

Cultural upheaval came with the 1960s, a new age dawned, and the Rolling Stones sang 'Time is on my side, yes it is'. And considering that they're still performing nearly half a century after their first gig in 1962, you'd have to say they were right.

An Interlude

The 'slow' Londoner might seem like a mythical species. After all, most people move away from the city in search of a slower pace of life. But one new Londoner punctures that paradox: **Carl Honoré**, the fast-talking, ice hockey-playing Canadian author of the international best-seller, *In Praise of Slow*. He has made London his home and explains how he has got to grips with the capital's pace:

'My view of slow is that slow is a frame of mind, and because of that you can be slow sitting in the middle St Pancras station just as you can be slow in an empty field in Dorset. It's how you approach a place. Do you arrive at each moment trying to do whatever it is you're doing as fast as possible or as well as possible? Do you try to inhabit that moment and squeeze as much as you can out of it or do you try to do several things at once?

'A city like London can be a double-edged sword. It can put a physical and emotional pressure on you to go faster. It might seem that it's easier to be slow in an obvious slow place, like that field in Dorset. But in some ways a city like London has advantages when it comes to slowing down. London is full of places that invite you to stop and stare. I've always tried to walk through London and not take the fast route, which is the Tube. Sometimes I'll just gratuitously stop a Tube station early or walk a couple of stops down streets I've never encountered before and I find it's a treasure trove of architectural follies. You notice the way the light falls on the façade of a Georgian terraced house at a certain time of day or you see a little private garden behind wrought-iron gates you've never seen before or you overhear a snippet of conversation. London is an Aladdin's cave of visual detail.

'A big part of slow is depth and texture and understanding that every object with meaning has a story behind it. It's when you stop to read about the city in a book like this and equip yourself before you go into a city that you get the most out of it. I feel that London in that way is hugely blessed. The flipside is that it is this extraordinary smorgasbord of temptations. You could have it all here – so people *want* to have it all.

'But having it all is just a recipe for hurrying it all. I think if you approach London in a much more slow spirit – "I'm going to take from the city the things that are magnificent and wonderful but I'm not going to try and take too much" – you have that gearshift going on. I can't think of a better place to slow down.

'London has the advantage of not being a modern city in the mould of Melbourne or Vancouver. It's a network of villages that grew up in a higgledy-piggledy fashion over the years, which means that when we go home I don't need to drive. My children go to school two streets away, we have two enormous parks flanking our enclave of Victorian houses, I do all my shopping on foot from

our local butcher, cheesemonger, fruit stall, baker. Those people all know my children's names and so you've got this incredibly slow register there but you also have this vortex of energy on your doorstep. It's how you use those two things.

'The world has a dysfunctional relationship with time. It's not a chiefly Anglo-Saxon phenomenon; it goes beyond work, to the way people eat, live and raise their children. The French now buy ready meals. Brazil and Argentina think they have to copy us.

'For me, slow is the idea that every thing, person, task has its own natural tempo, its own rhythm. What I'm trying to tackle is the notion that there is only one time, which is as fast as possible. I'm living pretty close to my rhythm, whereas to someone else what I'm doing may seem very fast.

'I used to feel rushed all the time. I was always looking at the clock; I was a card-carrying roadrunner. And now, I'm not. It's like I've changed the chip. Obviously, I've made concrete changes in my life but the bottom line is I'm living at my natural tempo. I talk fast, I'm quite dynamic, I play a lot of sports, I'm busy a lot of the time – but on my own terms now. One of the things I'm trying to knock down is the idea that slow is a dirty word, synonymous with torpid, lazy, unproductive; a taboo.

'How would I make London slower? I would come down like a ton of bricks on the car. I would make London as pedestrian and cycle friendly as Amsterdam. One of the things I feel an almost physical pain about is that London genuflects to the car at every turn. London's quite small actually. You can get from Paddington to Victoria in a few min-utes. Let's open it up to bicycles – not only will it change how people get around but it will change the whole tenor of the place. It will feel like people have reclaimed the city.

'There are so many different ways to think about how people move around London that shape the interior as well as the urban landscape. That's what cities do – they change the way we feel about ourselves, about people, about life. Cities of the future will have to be denser. Cities need to have time policies, on the use of time. They need to get away from the idea that everybody must do the same thing at the same time. That's at odds with our post-modern culture and creates misery. They can change the opening times for courts, schools, surgeries. That will open up the city.' ☙

Interview by Robin Barton

In the Moment

DAWN Ninety per cent of the population is asleep at 6am on a weekday (96 per cent at weekends), according to the Office of National Statistics. So if you get up for the dawn chorus you'll share London with, well, no more than 750,000 people. Some will be working in our six **wholesale food markets**, shipping the day's produce to restaurants and shops from the New Covent Garden fruit, veg and flower market in Nine Elms, Billingsgate fish market, Smithfield meat market and others. The markets open at 3am and are in full cry by 5am.

Alternatively, you can tune into that other dawn chorus; first to sing out are the **robins** (sharp, repeated trill), **thrushes** (chirp and whistle bursts) and **blackbirds** (fuller, rounder whistle). Next come the jaunty notes of the **tits** and the rather more mournful cry of **bullfinches**. And then all hell breaks loose with the screaming of the **jays** and the chatter of **magpies**. If your luck is really in you might catch something rare, like the visiting **chiffchaff** in summer, named after its distinctive song. At the end of it all, ponder on the wonderful fact that this chorus never ceases, moving across the earth with the early morning light, a wave of eternal melody.

Central London parks open at 5am, and there's a sense of witnessing hidden secrets as nocturnal creatures scurry back to their dens for the day. Our pick for watching undisturbed wildlife is **Regent's Park**. If you're lucky you may see hedgehogs' tracks in the dewy grass; this being one of their few remaining habitats in central London. Foxes dart around, especially in late spring when cubs are feeling bolder. It also has one of the most varied bird populations in the city, with 47 resident species and another 150 that flitter through; follow the circular Bird Walk from the northern end of Baker St for a privileged view. The park's tawny owls (also fond of Greenwich Park) will be making their last hunts, while in London's largest heronry by the boating lake the still, grey outlines stalk fish with an almost creepy patience.

The day's first horse-riding lessons are held at 7.15am in **Hyde Park** and the Household Cavalry limbers up here before trotting towards Whitehall at 7am. Buttons bright and thigh-high boots polished, this is a regular routine for the troopers.

MORNING The sun rises over the Thames estuary. Its first, low rays bounce off the water and a hazy light flatters London's bridges and towers. Photographers call this the golden hour and it is when you'll find Danny and Niamh from Thames River Adventures, sitting in their kayaks on the **Regent's Canal** soaking it all in.

Parliament Hill is just as good a sunrise, while South Londoners can climb Greenwich Hill and watch dawn's pinkish blush flow around the towers of Canary Wharf and lap at the foot of the hill; the elusive stillness is perfect for meditating on the day ahead.

Before breakfast drop into the **Turkish baths** (*www.aquaterra.org*) at Ironmonger Row, between Old Street and Angel tube stations. The tiled baths, with all their 1930s

charm, open at 6.30am and have marble slabs for body scrubbing or massage, three sweltering hot rooms and an icy plunge pool. In Hyde Park, the **Serpentine Swimmers Club** convenes at 7.30am for a constitutional crawl across the shallow water. We all wonder at our own mortality and time's effect on our bodies, but seeing an octogenarian diving into freezing water is curiously reassuring and inspiring. Wander across the park into the streets of London and watch the waking city stretch and yawn.

When weekend comes, ride your bike over to the **City** and swoop around its eerily deserted streets.

AFTERNOON Gather friends, fill a picnic basket, and mosey over to the **Kyoto Garden** in Holland Park, one of London's smallest and prettiest parks. With the waterfall burbling in the background unfurl your blanket, or take one of the benches around the park's Formal Gardens or in the Orangery, and the world's your oyster, or egg sandwich.

In the dog days of summer (we should be so lucky!) the cool marble floors, dim light and high ceilings of the **National Gallery** *(www.nationalgallery.org.uk)* are deliciously refreshing and relaxing (see p73 in See). Even if you've only got 10 minutes, there's something self-indulgent about gorging on Cezanne or Turner when the rest of the city is hard at work.

Flick through the pages of London's literary history with a visit to a second-hand bookshop, or ask an independent bookseller to recommend a new local talent. Find a tree to lean against and watch the city clock off as you read.

TWILIGHT The Kinks weren't wrong: there's a fine sunset from **Waterloo Bridge**. Upstream, the Houses of Parliament's stonework glows in the waning light and the day's last rays softly illuminate London's roofs, flagpoles and towers. You might be moved to take the last flight of the day on the **London Eye**; yes, it's a tourist magnet but seeing the dark Thames swirl through the illuminated city can remind us why we live in this great city.

At Evensong in **St Paul's Cathedral** *(daily 5pm, all welcome)*, the heavenly music swells inside Wren's domed masterpiece and inside any listener. For communion of a more natural sort, go **bat watching** at Dell Bridge and Serpentine Bridge in Hyde Park, on the Sackler Crossing across the lake in the Royal Botanic Gardens, Kew, or at the ponds on Hampstead Heath and around Kenwood House.

Rush-hour cyclists swarm out of the city centre like bats exiting a cave. Hyde Park's Victorian gaslights flicker into life and London's nightshift readies itself. The streets of the City are emptying of bankers but for the astronomers at the Royal Observatory in Greenwich the day is just beginning.

EVENING Sometimes all it takes to break out of the horological handcuffs is to wind the clock forward or back. What might seem mundane at one time suddenly becomes challenging, more interesting or downright exhilarating at another. The **Friday Night Ride** *(www. fridaynightride.com)* is an easy-going, if somewhat disorganised affair, where locals post a ride and anyone can join them. They tend to set off from a pub in the evening and can end up just about anywhere.

Time Keepers

From the moment we began to talk of timekeeping, it began to take hold of us, dragging us along at what feels like an increasingly urgent pace. But an afternoon at the Royal Observatory *(020 8858 4422; www.nmm.ac.uk)* is just the tonic for reminding us that time, measured in infinite aeons, is slower than it might seem.

Londoners weren't always ruled by time, a slippery commodity that was difficult to record and maintain. Time was – is – something natural, guided by the planets, the tides, the moon. Its passing was once measured by the age of trees; the turn of the seasons; the hours of daylight. But as adventurous mariners set sail for exotic lands, they required more accurate timekeeping – navigation by the skies was unreliable, not to mention a tad treacherous.

The Royal Observatory was built in 1675 crowning Greenwich Hill; from here, seafarers leaving London's docks could set their chronometers by the signal of a ball dropping down the flagstaff. Charles II would be chuffed to know that, thanks to his commission, every time and location around the world would thereafter be measured from London. Sailors began to calculate their positions using degrees of longitude from the Greenwich Meridian at 0 degrees – for every 15 degrees they travelled east or west, the local time changed by an hour. Science and seafaring were at their peak, modern times had begun, and London was at the centre of it all.

'Having the time' quickly became a status symbol. From the 1850s the Belville sisters set their pocket watch at the Observatory and toted it around the city, dispensing the correct time to their clients. Even after the BBC used the pips from Greenwich to mark the hour in 1924 and the Post Office launched its speaking clock service in 1935, the Belville time-checking service remained in business.

Even for those of who like to occasionally dance around the relentless march of time, there's something beautiful about the mechanical clocks and delicate brass navigational instruments exhibited in the National Maritime Museum, all dedicated to calibrating the passage of minutes, hours and days.

But the Royal Observatory inspires a greater understanding of time's true scale; it's measured by the birth and death of stars, by the speed light travels from the sun across the vast vacuum of space. Regular late-night events such as Winter Sky Watch and An Evening With the Stars use the Observatory's 28-inch telescope, the country's largest, to probe not just space but also our conception of time itself and what it means to each of us. ♞

THE HANDS BEHIND THE TIME

GREENWICH MEAN TIME, ON A CLOCK THAT'S NEAR IMPOSSIBLE TO READ

nature

KNOWING OUR PLACE

**IF YOU REALLY WANT SOLACE, PLEASURE AND DEEP
JOY, YOU'LL FIND IT IN THE NATURAL WORLD.**

" "

Sir David Attenborough

B eing in nature, even just *looking* at it, soothes stress. We know this instinctively, yet more and more academics are proving the point through science. So, it's tough luck living in Europe's largest city eh? Wrong. London has green spaces galore; plenty of native flora and fauna call it home; and the natural cycles of our surrounds set the rhythm for the city's pulse.

As a river city, London's natural life ebbs and flows with the tides as well as the seasons. Long the source of life in this corner of the country, the Thames also shapes our interior – describing oneself as living north or south of the river brings with it a parcel of associations. From the changes in weather to the spaces we play in, nature itself shapes our character and the way we fill our days.

Greeting Seasons

We share the weather's highs and lows, and our running commentary on the conditions connects us to nature and each other. As Stephen Fry once noted, we talk the heat up using Fahrenheit, but measure cold temperatures in the more miserable-sounding Celsius. Seasonal variation not only affects our mood, but also shapes our culture. It's not because of our balmy winters that we've become a world crucible for artistic expression; while long summer days coax pastimes from football to floriculture.

London is actually one of the driest, sunniest places in the UK, insulated from prevailing Atlantic weather fronts although first in line for a wintry Arctic sucker punch from Scandinavia. Seasonal changes can be subtle – more rain falls in August and September than in January and February – but there are certain days when you know a page has been turned, whether it's sighting the first daffodil in Hyde Park or seeing russet leaves twist and flutter from the plane trees. And every change in conditions encourages us to pause and reflect.

SPRING 'Spring is the new summer,' according to the Woodland Trust. In this topsy-turvy age when whales swim up the Thames and parakeets breed in London trees, the first buds of the new year still thrill us with the promise of new life. We shrug off winter's embrace and look forward to strolls around parks and al fresco pints at riverside pubs.

For some, spring's starting gun is sounded by the annual Oxford vs Cambridge Boat Race in March; for others it comes when the first canary-yellow daffodils sprout. The speckles of colour on grey city streets remind us that anything can happen in the next few months, and the possibility of warmth melts the last of that winter misery. April is as likely as July to be the hottest month so we take our chances where we find them, with sandals and strappy dresses at the ready from Easter onwards.

Of course, for every day of sunny succour, there will be a day of rain, which always seems more drenching when dressed in our new season's optimism. The key is to never underestimate London's weather; James Smith probably figured this out when he opened London's first umbrella shop in 1830, still standing at 53 New Oxford St today.

SUMMER We live for summer, which is why we get ahead of ourselves and bask in April sunshine – it could, plausibly, be the only sun of the year. But when summer does arrive, however fleeting it may be, it brings sweltering Tube trains, tourists dangling their feet in fountains and *Standard* headlines screaming '31°C!' – and no sooner does the city heat up than we wish for it to cool down. It's not just the weather that is fickle.

Office workers, like spawning salmon, race for the nearest patch of greenery and flop, gasping, on the grass. Give in to temptation and take an extra half hour break – nothing picks up the afternoon like a loll on a lawn or snooze in the sun as the lunchtime rush

THE GRASS IS GREENER AT MUDCHUTE CITY FARM IN THE SHADOW OF CANARY WHARF

swarms about you. Stolen from time and routine, it's the easiest and most vitamin D-enriched way to slow down.

Summers change the way we dress – more colour, less material – what music we listen to, where we hang out and how well we seem to remember. Make hay while you can.

AUTUMN Autumn is as colourful as spring, but with added texture. Great drifts of magenta, bronze and golden leaves pile up in parks and on pavements, begging to be kicked through but it's magical to be caught in a light shower of leaves as they flutter and fall.

Phenologists (people who study the seasons) note that trees are clinging onto their leaves as late as December these days as our climate changes. Summer that stretches into September and October is no bad thing for us, but London's few remaining swifts must get confused about when to migrate for Africa for winter and the bats of Hampstead Heath need to rearrange their hibernation plans.

The hotter the summer, the bigger autumn's thunderstorms, and the drama of stormy clouds unleashing lightning and rain on a hot city is thrilling; get outside and watch the way stormy light turns the city into a scene by Turner. Of course, that's not the only drama that unfolds under the autumn skies; festivals of all persuasions carry on into September and October as we try to slow the inexorable march of winter.

We put off knitting that winter scarf or buying that winter coat, knowing we'll need it but refusing to let the inevitable encroach on our *now*. But the clocks go forward at the end of October, darkness seeps through the late afternoon streets, and we submit.

WINTER The heavy snowfalls of winter 2009 transformed the city and its people, an emphatic reminder of how we can be shaped and inspired by the seasons. Armies of snowmen invaded parks and grinning children whizzed down slopes on tea trays instead of sitting in class. Strangers smiled at each other during the strangely euphoric week. 'Wasn't that amazing?' agrees Carl Honoré. 'Maybe some of that *joie de vivre* could be brought back. It was very telling. Children were out playing in our street where parents normally have them on leashes.'

Winter normally turns us into homebodies. Perhaps we're mimicking the leafless trees, and the hibernation patterns of squirrels, bats and other chilly critters that hide in them. We ration our outdoor hours, with bitter temperatures limiting us to hurried transit. But winter gloom is only a state of mind; embrace the way the season slows down your natural rhythm and savour the simple pleasures of weekend papers, sipping tea and Sunday roasts. Take solace in the close company of family or in the pages of a great book. Hang the holiday and find your escape in a warming nip of whisky or a handful of roasted chestnuts, even the invigoration of that first tooth-chattering breath of morning.

London streets look ever so romantic through the mist and rain; pull on your wellies and enjoy them with a splash. Lace up your ice skates and imagine an even chillier London, if you can, when locals celebrated the freezing over of the Thames with donkey rides and football on ice at Frost Fairs until 1814.

Smile with every snowdrop and know that you'll appreciate spring all the more because you lived winter to the full.

Green Spaces

'Everybody needs beauty as well as bread, places to play in and pray in, where nature may heal and cheer and give strength to body and soul.' John Muir's words address our spiritual need for green spaces. Nature replenishes our spiritual bank for free and we're amazingly lucky to have London's many parks in which to nourish our souls. London, of course, likes to claim titles; the biggest city in Europe is also the greenest. Don't believe us? You only have to approach by air, or look east across the city from Kew or Richmond; we're surrounded by more green than grey.

Public space has always been important for the wellbeing of communities, but with London's absurdly high-density dwelling, it's now more vital than ever. Fortunately we're blessed with over 150 nature reserves, parks and gardens woven between the city's streets. Whether we're strolling through a park, contemplating the view, deadheading in the garden or even picking a few herbs from the window box, nature is just the tonic for our increasingly harried lives. Even people who work in the equivalent of windowless dungeons only need to incorporate a park, garden or green space into the commute or lunch break to feel healthier and happier. People don't flourish under fluorescent lighting. If the Himalayan Alps screen saver isn't working, go for a walk.

PARKS London's parks draw us to them, removing us temporarily from the stresses of urban living. The Royal Parks are where it all begins. The oldest in central London, **St James' Park** was founded by King Henry VIII as a convenient place for a post-work hunt. The sylvan area around the ponds is shady in summer and has the added entertainment of royal pelicans patrolling the water. **Regent's Park** is more ornamental; there's no resisting the heady scent when the Rose Garden's 30,000 roses are in bloom. The Open Air Theatre is in action from late May throughout the summer, and is thankfully distanced from the new Wildlife Garden, recently added to attract birds and insects. To glimpse the new breed of royalty, head to **Hampstead Heath**, natural habitat of the A-list celebrity.

The preserve of locals, the lesser-known green spaces can make it easier to connect with nature without the pomp and pageantry. In the borough of Tower Hamlets, **Victoria Park** attracts anglers and birdwatchers to arguably east London's favourite green space (**London Fields** vies for attention), now on the edge of the site of the 2012 Olympic Games. The park, where the Hertford Union Canal meets Regent's Canal, is a venue for outdoor theatre and concerts, weaving normal life into nature with exhilarating positive effect. Further along the Regent's Canal, the **Camley Street Natural Park** is one of London's newest nature reserves. Once a coal yard for the railways, the community-run project introduces local children to creatures such as bats, amphibians and birds.

From Richmond Park to Epping Forest, south London is bursting with green, breathing oases, any of which are worth a stroll. With its labyrinths of leafy glades and tangles of heather and hedgerows, **Wimbledon Common** is an untamed favourite. Spare thanks for the Wombles; it always seems impossibly pristine. Just south of Brixton, **Brockwell Park** is calm and unruffled until the Lambeth Country Show brings it to life with the smells of joints and jerk chicken. With views of Canary Wharf, the Gherkin and the London Eye from the top of the hill, you get a sense of being in London but not stifled by the city. Perspective, er, man.

London runners are blessed with parks for playgrounds. 'I find many of my best ideas come to me after a run,' says slowcoach Carl Honoré, 'because I've switched off, I'm listening to the birds, I'm smelling different things. There's a meditative quality. Any kind of rhythmic activity, like knitting, has this effect.'

One run really suits our pace. Every autumn the London Tree-athlon (*www.tree-athlon. org*) brings tree-lovers together in **Battersea Park** for a breezy 5km run, rewarding them at the end with a native sapling to take home and plant. The race raises money for urban conservation projects, and entrants are invited to make 'tree wishes' – statements of hope for the future of London's trees.

Gardens

If an Englishman's home is his castle, then his garden is his park. However small the space, if it can be cultivated and manicured it will be, as the **Museum of Garden History** *(Lambeth Palace Rd; www.gardenmuseum.org.uk)* illustrates. Among the order of flowerbeds, trimmed hedges and neat lawns, tranquillity prevails.

'There is something very slowing about nature,' Carl Honoré tells us. 'One of the things I do while walking around London is to go into those little private gardens in Kensington, Chelsea, and sit on a bench. They're wonderful, they're a little oasis and what you hear most, rather than a ringtone, is birdsong.' These exclusive corners are as serene as the back seat of a Bentley, but usually protected by black railings and locked gates. Fortunately, we hoi polloi can scramble inside once a year during the **Open Garden Squares Weekend** *(www.opensquares. org)* in June.

For something different, look up. With space at such a premium, gardens in the sky have taken root. Gardener David Lewis is in charge of one of the most exotic and surprising spaces in London: **Kensington Roof Gardens** *(access via Derry St, www.roofgardens.com)* has several themed gardens 100ft above High St Kensington, including a Spanish garden inspired by Granada's Alhambra. David's companions on the roof are Bill and Ben, a pair of flamingos. Japan was the inspiration for the roof garden at the **School of Oriental and African Studies** off Russell Square. Geometric shapes and straight, raked lines contend with the rambling wisteria and lemon thyme of the roof space. You can visit the garden whenever the Brunei Gallery *(www.soas.ac.uk)* is open, and it's also part of the annual London Festival of Architecture.

MANY MODES OF SLOW IN GREENWICH PARK

An Orderly Kew

Right, by now we've established our good fortune that wherever we live or work in London, we're never far from a patch of green. But imagine living in London and inside one of the world's most spectacular gardens. Meet Nigel Taylor, curator of the Royal Botanical Gardens in Kew *(020 8332 5655; www.kew.org)*.

'It's certainly a privilege and I hope my family don't take it for granted,' he laughs. Since becoming a botanic garden in 1841, Kew has collected more than 30,000 plant species from around the world. 'It's southwest London's green lung and has a huge positive impact on the physical and mental health of Londoners,' says Nigel. The gardens were as popular in the Victorian age as they are now: 'Back then there was a big push to get people out of the dirty cities and into green spaces, and visitor numbers rocketed after the railway arrived.'

I'm keen to visit something in particular; a tree that was thought extinct until rediscovered in 1994, something so rare that there are fewer than 100 examples surviving in the wild. But Nigel's not having any of it, insisting on taking me on a tour first.

'Kew is an iceberg,' he says. 'The bit you see is only a tiny part. There's a much bigger scientific endeavour behind the scenes; the Herbarium, the Millennium Seed Bank, which will hold 25 per cent of the world's plant species by 2020, and the finest botanical library in the world.' In 2003 Kew was made a World Heritage Site for its role in

distributing its expertise around the world. Crops such as tea, coffee and rubber were propagated from the gardens and even Australian sheep farming was kick-started with a flock of Kew's prized merino sheep (obtained illicitly from Spain).

The most arresting view in Kew is from the 18-metre high walkway, which opened in 2008 and zig-zags for 200 metres through the treetops in a Capability Brown-designed arboretum. 'Look east across London and you see trees not buildings,' says Nigel, 'there are huge expanses of the capital that are not concrete jungles.' The weathered steel structure, blending beautifully with the autumnal trees, has a lifespan of at least 500 years – 'We'll be under water long before then,' Nigel half-jokes – and is strong enough to hold a fallen tree and designed to sway with the wind.

Above the trees, the most remarkable realisation (or really a re-realisation of the flipping obvious) is that the leaves are actually shiny, as opposed to the matt finish we normally see when looking at their undersides. It's just as unusual to be at eye-level with birds and among the species here are three varieties of woodpecker, tawny and little owls, sparrowhawks and merlins, not to mention seven species of bat.

Whatever the season, Kew has something to enjoy. The famous Palm House, opened in 1848, is heated to 25°C daily and in winter, when the outside temperature is struggling to stay in the positive, the condensation inside is so rapid that it rains. Where else in London can you have a tropical downpour in January?

From February to May five million bulbs flower, a truly magical time to visit says Nigel, who nominates his favourite late spring spot as the 17th-century Queen's Garden behind the palace.

The first May Bank Holiday is the busiest weekend of the year but it's easy to escape the crowds in the Rhododendron Dell, the Redwood Grove and especially in the semi-natural Conservation Zone in the grounds of Queen Charlotte's Cottage (with bluebell wood), the most tranquil part of Kew's southwest. On summer evenings, visitors watch bats from the Zen-like Sackler Crossing over the lake.

But belying the slowness of my pursuit, I'm getting a little impatient to see the object of my visit: a Wollemi Pine. Sir David Attenborough planted one in a cage near the main gate in 2005, a reference to its rarity. But there's another, near the Evolution House, that is finally within reach. Standing a couple of feet taller than me, with flat, waxy fronds, this is a species that has survived everything time could throw at it – dinosaurs, ice ages and meteorites. It now has us to contend with.

'It was found when an Australian Parks and Wildlife Officer abseiled into a hard-to-reach canyon near Sydney,' says Nigel. 'He didn't recognise the tree and a sample of it dumbfounded experts. Remarkably, they could only identify it by matching it with a fossil. The tree is so scarce that location of the canyon where it grows is a closely guarded secret.'

It's a plaintive experience, touching a species that has existed unchanged for at least 90 million years. Global propagation looks to have safeguarded the species but, as Nigel notes, its survival is now in our hands. It was thought lost forever and its rediscovery has been described as the botanical find of the 20th century. The name 'Wollemi' provides sound advice for a slow tour of Kew Gardens: 'look around you.' ᛰ

Wild London

Apparently the Thames has been flowing for some 450,000 years. Time whittled away the banks we now call home, seeing ice sheets, then tundra and clambering native woodland. And then our ancestors arrived 40,000 years ago and slowly started clearing the lot. Wild greenery gave way to farmland, and eventually the urban jungle we now know.

In Greenwich, Oxleas Wood is an 8000-year-old reminder of what London may have looked like when untamed ancient woodland proliferated. Further south still, Sydenham Hill Wood is the last stand of the Great North Wood. These places offer a plaintive glimpse into a London before London. Rich tracts of sessile oak and hornbeam shelter ancient buildings and thriving wildlife. Bats, elsewhere threatened, prosper; frogs, newts and toads live in harmony with native birds; and incredibly, all three species of local woodpecker still breed.

ON LAND

Some of our wild creatures are native, others introduced; all enjoy the hospitality of the city's oldest inhabitants, the trees. Oaks, elders and birch line suburban streets, while other species are more localised, like the 400-year-old sweet chestnuts in Greenwich Park and Green Park's black poplars, which are Britain's rarest native trees and recognised by their gnarled trunks.

We'll begin with a story; the London Wildlife Trust calls it 'a tale of two squirrels'. London's conifers were once filled with the cheering sight of red squirrels, but since their grey cousins were brought across the Atlantic at the end of the 19th century, they've all but disappeared. Grey squirrels have taken exceptionally well to their new home, feasting on suburban streets at all hours. Frankly, they're opportunists who've reached almost pestilent proportions, but we can't begrudge them entirely – after more than a century, we have to admit they're locals now (plus, don't hate us, but when you catch them munching down on seeds they really are terribly cute).

That's why we were pleased (well…) when the Trust told us the fate of reds in London is not actually dependent on grey numbers, but rather on the destruction of habitat – and it's not the squirrels who are to blame for that. One of the best places to see grey squirrels up close is Brompton Cemetery, darting for scraps between the headstones.

Antlered residents have left a 'browse line' in the trees at Richmond. There's something nostalgic about glimpsing majestic **red deer**, Britain's largest land mammal, grazing in southwest London; it's a calmer sight than the kind of stags prowling the rest of the city. Several herds live in Richmond Park and rutting stags can be heard bellowing in the autumn. They share the park with **fallow deer**, which cool themselves in summer by wading in the shallow streams.

Wherever you live in London you will have heard, if not seen, a city **fox**. Their unearthly shriek is ever more common in the capital with an estimated 15,000 foxes living within the M25. They're not entirely welcome, ripping bin bags open and chasing

BUCKING THE TREND IN RICHMOND PARK

cats; one even wandered into the Office shoe shop on Portobello Rd in January 2007 for a snooze among the shoes. Even the foxes have adapted to the conditions in London it seems, being more brazen and street smart than their country cousins.

UNDERWATER Like veins stretching through our heart, our rivers and canals have shaped and sustained us for centuries, providing food, fuelling industry, nurturing imagination and dictating sprawl. Whether we explore their banks, their currents or the historic tales written in their murky depths, they allow us to reflect on London and on the way we, too, flow through the landscape.

The **River Lea**, running across the East End, follows the course of London's industrial past and present, feeding into tanners, smokers and factories along its length. It was once the main highway for transporting Norfolk barley to London breweries, and is now passing right through the new Olympic village. South, the **River Wandle** meanders through lakes, wetlands and towns founded around its mills, at about the same easy pace as the fishermen taking to its recently rejuvenated banks, joined early evenings by herons and coots.

The city's waterways seem to be getting cleaner by the year, attracting back some remarkable creatures. No recovery has been more impressive than the once-fetid **Thames**, which is now attracting **wild otters** that were introduced into the River Lea. Common and grey **seals** have been spotted at Tower Bridge, their dog-like faces bobbing in the water. **Salmon** and **trout**, amazingly, have returned to the Thames. But not all wild

water creatures are discerning; in 2009 a colony of **water voles** – more cute than clever – chose a sewage plant in east London as their new home and, for their own safety, had to be lured away with carrots and apples.

The greatest menace in the Thames is a growing infestation of **Chinese Mitten crab**, a plate-sized crustacean that feasts on native species and damages river banks with its burrowing. It's edible, so if you want to help preserve the health of our iconic waterway, get out your crabbing poles and start getting creative in the kitchen.

And while you're doing your bit at home, step into the back garden, indeed one of the best places to get up close with nature at any time. The happy cackle of common frogs has been on the wane in recent years (crazy ringtones notwithstanding) as wetland area has disappeared, but their saviour has been the humble garden pond.

So get digging. Not only will it help these threatened creatures, but it can also bring much joy to our own lives – who hasn't been fascinated by their alluring metamorphosis? 'It demonstrates evolution compressed into just a few weeks and it sparks our imagination,' said Sir David Attenborough in 2008 (Year of the Frog, incidentally), when he launched **Amphibian Ark** *(www.amphibianark.org)*, a worldwide breeding, conservation and education project.

IN THE SKY Scrawny, scrappy and wearing dirt-friendly uniforms of grey, the urban **pigeon** is an opportunist. Only the camera-wielding tourists notice them and we tend not to give them a second glance as long as they're quick enough to get out of our path. But, next time, look at a kit of pigeons being fed illicitly by a tourist or swarming over some rubbish and you'll see a complex, greedy, Darwinian society revelling in abundance. Not a bad metaphor for the city's brand of capitalism.

Fortunately, there are more exciting birds to spot, some of which have pigeons for lunch. Two of London's famous feathered residents are Misty and Bert, a pair of **peregrine falcons** who call Tate Modern's brick tower home. The Royal Society for the Protection of Birds (RSPB) trains its telescopes on the pair on summer afternoons, from a perch by Millennium Bridge. **Sparrowhawks** have also long been used to clear an area of pigeons and often dart through hedges and gardens – they're small and grey with yellow talons and the large yellow-rimmed eyes of a predator.

'Greater London is home to more than two hundred different species of birds, with a variety of lost or waylaid migrants making regular appearances,' says Tim Webb of the RSPB. 'There are iridescent **kingfishers** on Hampstead Heath's ponds and lanky, grey **herons** in Hyde Park. The Thames acts as a wildlife motorway, leading the migrating birds deep inland.'

In the right frame of mind, your daily commute can be transformed from a grind into a bird-watching adventure. 'On the tubes and trains our track sidings are great places for wildlife,' suggests Tim. 'On the buses, check out trees, parks and gardens for **finches**, **tits** and **jays**. And if you walk or cycle, your chances of seeing birds is much improved.' You don't need any special equipment – just a keen eye and a slow sensibility. And according to Tim, as a result of climate change there will be new species of birds to see over coming decades so you might be the first person in Britain to spot a male Indian peafowl, a bird we picked entirely at random because it has a mildly amusing name.

At the Wildfowl and Wetland Trust's **London Wetland Centre** *(020 8409 4400; Queen Elizabeth's Walk, Barnes; www.wwt.org.uk)*, catch a glimpse of the endangered **Hawaiian goose**. 'If I'm honest, they're a slightly daft species,' says biologist and warden Idris Bhatti. The geese were tragically unprepared for predators introduced by colonists to Hawaii, and so trusting that they walked right up to human hunters. Numbers were down to 30 worldwide in the 1950s but more than 200 have been bred by the WWT, though it remains one of the world's rarest birds.

There's something magical about catching a rare glimpse of a **swift** silhouetted against the sunset, but our sources tell us we might be mistaken; more likely it's a **noctule**, the largest of London's **bats**. Don't be disappointed, they're just as enchanting: as the **London Bat Group** *(LBG; www.londonbats.org.uk)* points out, they've been hanging around for some 50 million years (the group can guide you towards some enthralling bat-spotting walks around the capital).

Although numbers are declining due to habitat loss – noctules are terribly choosy about which woodpecker or rot hole they'll roost in – they're still widespread. Far more common are **pipistrelles**, not least because they've managed to hang on in the most urbanised areas, roosting in walls and eaves. This tiny bat has a wingspan of 20cm and weighs a mere four grams, yet it can scoff more than 3000 insects in a night. You'll spot them feeding in woodland, over water, in gardens and hedgerows, even feasting on the insects that gather around streetlights.

Urban Birding

Three men in hats and dark coats, with telescopes and binoculars, outside a high-security prison at dawn – what could possibly go wrong?

We're on the patch of scrubland outside Wormwood Scrubs with David Lindo, aka The Urban Birder *(www.theurbanbirder. com)*. He has been birdwatching daily on this patch for almost 17 years and has even given a talk at the prison ('Birds?!' exclaimed one lag. 'But you're black!').

Hemmed in by industrial estates, terraced housing and the barbed wire-topped walls of the Scrubs, this flat patch of common land seems an unlikely spot for communing with nature. But David, who is chairman of the Ornithological section of the London Natural History Society, thinks otherwise.

'Birds don't know this is a city,' he says. 'You have to imagine that this is a wilderness, that people don't exist and that buildings are cliffs. There's more to life in cities than people realise. (Although I wouldn't advise people to come here in the evening when there are a few dodgy characters about.)'

On a cold, bright Sunday morning in November, we start David's regular circuit in the southwest corner of Wormwood Scrubs, making our way towards an embankment thrown up when the Eurostar terminal was constructed at St Pancras. I have no trouble identifying the crows strutting around the common but David's keen eye sees much more. 'That's a skylark,' he says, as a brown shape flits across the corner of my vision.

'That bird with its back to us is a dunnock. Hear that tss-tss-tss? That's a goldcrest.'

'I've always been good at recognising birds, ever since I was a child,' says David. 'I memorised the stats in a book about European birds.' At school – he lived two miles north of where we're standing – he got a bit of stick from other pupils, naturally. 'My reply was always, "I'm doing something different. What are you doing?" I admit that I'm an anorak – but a Gucci anorak.'

He gives talks, leads bird-watching tours in cities around the world and has presented on the BBC several times. 'It's hard to convince people that they don't need to leave the city to see some amazing birds,' he says. 'I try to tell people the back story to every bird – if they see a swift I tell them, for example, that the bird spent the first four years of its life on the wing (never stopping).'

Although we've missed the best birding month in London, September, when migrants are busy arriving or departing, there's still plenty to see. A kestrel hovers over some long grass – left uncut by the council at David's request to encourage wildlife – then dives towards its prey; only the horn of a freight train leaving King's Cross reminds me we're in deepest west London. Instead of 'a bunch of seagulls', I recognise three of four different species of gulls.

'We had our first osprey fly over recently,' says David, 'that was a "wow". For the last five years I've seen a cuckoo here. Nightingales are quite scarce but every year we get

one passing through. Hearing it sing puts the hairs on the back of your neck up.'

'Being an urban birder means you look at everything because there are fewer birds. My attitude is to expect to see everything and nothing. No urban birder leaves home without binoculars. Seeing things out of context gives you sharper eyes,' he says, proving the point when he spots a black redstart on a Berwick St rooftop; there are fewer than 100 breeding pairs in the UK.

As we walk along the edge of the embankment towards an untidy copse of hawthorn, greeting dog walkers and other birdwatchers, David makes a case for enjoying nature through more than the prism of a television screen. 'You lose part of your humanity if you get disconnected from nature. It's vital for sanity. I'm always birding, it's part of my spirit, it's grounded me. I come here every morning and I feel so privileged to be part of a greater process.'

But isn't birdwatching for the obsessive-compulsive, the ticker of lists? No, apparently that's twitching. Birdwatchers are a completely different species, happy to just sit back and wait. 'It's easy to get into. Don't worry about identifying every bird you see, just enjoy it. In this day and age people want instant gratification – they want to be overnight experts.'

Not me; I find that I'm content to watch goldfinches and pippets dart in and out of brambles, oblivious to us and the day's first jets streaming towards Heathrow. For a few moments we watch life lived to their rules, and distractions and worries recede. Perhaps the 60 prisoners inspired by David's talk at Wormwood Scrubs get the same feeling when they watch the swifts swooping outside their windows every May, and might make more of this opportunity if they could. In the distance a crow mobs the kestrel, they twist and turn together in the city skyline, as the sun rises high over east London and the first Sunday footballers arrive.

Robin Barton

work

IF WE HAVE TO

66

I LIKE WORK: IT FASCINATES ME.
I CAN SIT AND LOOK AT IT FOR HOURS.

Jerome K Jerome

99

George Bernard Shaw predicted technology would lead to an age of leisure, where by 2000 we would only need to work two hours a day. What the heck happened? Work is a modern addiction: thanks to smartphones, Wi-Fi and email we're always on call, wherever we are, whatever time of the day. Britons already work the longest hours in Europe and, according to the Trades Union Congress, five million of us do unpaid overtime. It's no wonder we so often define ourselves by our jobs; we're important, you know, because we're 'needed by work'.

London's the engine room for all this work, and it's largely the reason we're all here. But this chapter is a reminder that we're working to live and not the other way around. Slow isn't just something to appreciate when you clock off, but a whole new relationship to the clock itself.

Every Working Hour

If the global financial crisis taught us one thing, it's that there's more to life than work. As author Alain de Botton notes, 'For most of the recent past our efforts at improvement have focused on increasing our wealth. Now we will have to find other goals to aim for in our work.' When banking and law offer no more job security than poetry or carpentry, as de Botton puts it, why not do something you love, something that fulfils and rewards the soul rather than the wallet? Entrepreneurialism, collaboration, innovation and creativity will be stronger for it.

Hard times remind us of the real value of things, and the importance of connections with fellow humans and the natural world. 'I never use the phrase work-life balance,' we were told by Carl Honoré, author of the groundbreaking *In Praise of Slow*. 'I'd ask why work should be separate from your life – as far as possible the two things should be conflated. You should approach both with the same slow spirit.

'A big part of getting the slow idea across,' Carl suggests, 'is knocking on the head the idea that slow is this little oasis in your agenda when you suddenly become very Zen and you're having home-grown food, then you get back on the crazy treadmill. Slow is about your whole relationship with time. Embracing your inner tortoise is easiest in a food market, a more natural fit when you're on holiday, but it's harder to get your head around in the office. But I would argue that if it can happen it needs to happen in all those spheres.'

There's a story from a leading London law firm where a trainee lawyer gets up from his desk at 10.30pm and puts on his coat, only to be met by his boss asking, 'cold, is it?' Start by leaving on time rather than feeling obliged to be the last person sitting at the screen. Follow the old adage to work smarter, not harder (it will benefit you and your employer). And do, for goodness sake, take time off.

SMARTER Applying the principles of slow (at least our principles) to the concept of work is not about just going with the flow and getting a bit of cash. On the contrary, it's about being organised so you don't waste precious time, and about taking every precaution against tasks becoming tedious.

Plan, prepare, communicate efficiently, delegate, get things done on time and finish projects strongly (rather than when you're frazzled and liable to make mistakes).

Recognise your point of 'diminishing returns, when you're possibly doing more harm than good and would be better off going for a walk, taking a rest or just letting your hair down. And remember, some of the greatest breakthroughs – ones that actually made a difference in the world – came about not when people like Isaac Newton and Charles Darwin were toiling tirelessly at their desks but rather when one was sitting under a tree and the other sitting out enjoying his garden.

BREAKFAST Londoners used to do breakfast so well – there were caffs especially for market workers, caffs for cabbies and 'cafes' for City workers. Some years later the first Starbucks opened – and the rest is a sorry history of frothy coffees in paper cups. As one London Review of Breakfasts *(londonreviewofbreakfasts.blogspot. com)* correspondent, Hashley Brown, cries: 'Where did all the breakfasts go, succour to so many brilliant young minds?'

Rushed mornings jolt us into breakneck days, while breakfast is like a long, deep breath that prepares mind, body and soul for the day ahead. Suss out at a cosy caff on your route to work or make time at home for a newspaper and a nourishing snack. If you can't stomach a Full English, at least pause for a moment rather than eating on the move. And if you find science more palatable than slow philosophy, you need breakfast to replenish glucose levels so your brain works better, to be more relaxed and to stop you binging later.

LUNCH Gordon Gekko had it wrong; it's skipping lunch that is for wimps. The lunch-avoider says, 'Look at me – I'm simply too busy to even have a sandwich at my desk'. But what others see is someone too disorganised to get their work done in order to take time out for an enriching break.

If you're lucky enough to work near a market, rejoice! If a sandwich shop is your staple, find a patch of greenery nearby and savour every lingering mouthful. Now and then, bring in a home-cooked meal to share with a few close colleagues. Reclaim the lunch hour – yes, 60 glorious minutes that belong to you – and switch off. This is a time to chew over ideas, forge connections with others, or just lie back and close your eyes. Go for a walk. Sit under a tree and read. Catch a lunchtime concert in one of the city's churches, or gorge on a little bit of art at a nearby gallery. Shop – and no, errands don't count. Meditate, sketch, take a yoga class – do *whatever you like.*

Tension Breakers

- Refresh your mind with a 30-minute meditation in the office led by experts from Covent Garden's Inner Space *(www.innerspace.org.uk)*.
- Emergency foot massage is dished out by a team of on-call reflexologists in the City; you might do well with extra attention to the tips of the toes, which correspond to the brain and head *(www.footse.co.uk)*.
- The Laughter Network *(www.laughternetwork.co.uk)* hosts lunch-hour or half-day workshops in mirth; it de-stresses and improves communication.
- The Spiral Tree *(www.thespiraltree.com)* offers one-day small-group relaxation seminars, teaching stress management techniques and morale-boosters.
- Improve your outlook with Reiki Visions *(www.reikivisions.co.uk)*; the holistic therapy aids physical, mental and emotional healing.

INTO THE FOG: COMMUTERS MARCH ACROSS LONDON BRIDGE

FREEDOM

WE NEED
CHANGE

2008

Ways to Work

The commute brackets the day. You can't always control what happens between the brackets, but you can make choices about the commute that will affect your wellbeing and inner calm. Who's ever lamented the decision to cycle as they stream past congestion charge traffic, or longed for the Tube while strolling to the office?

BY FOOT Walking to work might seem mad if you live in Mile End and work in the West End, but London, believe it or not, is a walker's city. Ancient roads, timeless views, intriguing shortcuts: it's all here. You don't have to walk the whole way, just hop off the Tube a few stops early so you can pass a favourite cafe or catch sunlight hitting a particular spot.

Our friend David Webb, a banker, always crosses Hyde Park on his way to the office in Mayfair. 'I find it the most important time of the day for arranging my thoughts,' he says. 'It's almost meditative and I love seeing how the park changes throughout the year, from burned grass in the summer to icicles hanging off the Serpentine gallery in winter. It helps me start the day with a steady heart rate rather than after the stress of a Tube journey. I also know exactly how long it takes me to walk; public transport is more unpredictable. On the way back, my walk helps me digest the day.'

BY PEDAL Cycling has boomed over recent years and while provision for cyclists isn't great – Oh! To pedal through Copenhagen or Amsterdam! – it is improving, with more workplaces offering secure lock-ups and changing facilities. The Ride to Work scheme, which began in 2005, can even save you 50 percent off the cost of a new bike.

Simon O'Hagan, editor and Cyclo-therapy columnist at *The Independent*, cycles to or from work pretty much every day from his home in Queen's Park to Canary Wharf. 'I look at my diary for the week,' he tells us. 'One day a week I drive to work with clean clothes, then I'll probably make six journeys by bike, then drive back with the bike and a car full of dirty clothes at the end of the week. My sense of bodily wellbeing is off the scale. It keeps me in shape and enables me to eat what I feel like. Mentally, it's all about escaping. It's a great way to wind down at the end of a stressful day. You reach a blissful state of relaxation and concentration.'

First-time cycle commuters are often put off by the traffic, and it's true dodgy driving confronts every London cyclist. 'I'd be lying if I said I was never scared,' says Simon, 'but the more you cycle in London and the more you get used to the conditions, the safer you feel. It helps doing the same journey all the time: I know where every manhole cover is and where the surface changes. I have hotspots of danger, like a colour-coded commute.' Is he mad for not wearing a helmet? 'I've come to believe, very strongly, that it puts the onus on the cyclist defending themselves, whereas it should be the car driver's responsibility not to injure a cyclist. It's about fighting back. It works for me; a helmet alienates me from the experience I'm seeking. The whole beauty of the bicycle is the freedom and taking control of your destiny.

'I don't use an iPod but I do listen to a digital radio,' he confesses. 'On the way to work I listen to the *Today* programme and on the way back I listen to *Radcliffe and Maconie* on Radio 2. Getting on the bike at the end of the day and listening to that is just heaven.' Sure, he mightn't hear the city's natural beats, but you could argue the BBC presenters are as much the sound of London as traffic. At any rate, it's Simon's choice; when cycling, he gets to set his own rhythm.

BY WATER While the daily human tide is sluiced down through the Underground's pipes, the slow-moving Thames ushers a cool, calm alternative. How many commuters crossing London's bridges wish they could hop in a boat and drift downstream for the day? Well, according to instructor Kevin Burke of the Westminster Boating Base opposite the old Battersea Power Station, they could do just that, in a kayak, dinghy or rowing boat. The cool breeze on your face, the sky pink from the sunrise, the burbles and splashes of the water under your prow – it might sound a bit, well, wet, but it's surely a more idyllic start the day than the dusty, crowded Tube. What's more, you'll be self-powered, carbon neutral, fitter and less stressed.

The requirements are a little bit more complicated: somewhere to tie up your vessel, a place to change clothes and, unless you work on the river or canals, a way of getting from dock to desk. Try it out with Thames River Adventures *(020 8361 3009; www.thames-riveradventures.co.uk)* before splashing out on a craft of your own. More likely, however, you'll be taking one of the riverboat services along the Thames. As one commuter puts it: 'Commuting by water puts me in a more relaxed frame of mind. This is one of London's best-kept secrets.' An added bonus is that you can take a bicycle on board; try doing that on the Northern Line!

BY OYSTER What, you ask; now you're going to tell us London's public transport is slow? We love to bemoan it but, seriously, the city's bus, train and underground network is one of the most comprehensive in the world. Mix it up and try a new route; it might set you back 10 minutes, but it'll open up a whole new city.

Get your head out of the freesheet and use this 'me' time creatively: plot a novel, sketch a cityscape through a bus window, or learn a new language. It's becoming less unusual to see people knitting on the Tube or crocheting on the bus. If it's too early for your creativity to kick in, do the unthinkable and smile (at least with your eyes). 'Cities are full of people and we move through them too fast,' argues Carl Honoré. 'Do you catch peoples' eye, just to have a little more human contact? I think that's coming back.'

Break the downward stare and notice the art deco stylings of Charles Holden's stations on the Northern Line, the sci-fi steel of Sir Norman Foster's Canary Wharf station, or Isambard Brunel's Paddington Station with its Victorian ironwork and airy platforms. And athough there's little to lift the soul at one of the oldest stations, London Bridge, why not cross the road to Borough Market for a change?

WISDOM PURLED FROM I KNIT LONDON'S GERALD ALLT: STICK TO SMALLER PROJECTS ON THE TUBE

Good Company

The world of work is changing. Where once a job for life meant a 9 to 5 routine and gradual promotion, today the corporate ladder is more of a corporate lattice and contractors and freelancers are taking the place of the full-time employee. Is it still possible to find a slow workplace in our hectic capital?

From the 16th to the 19th centuries Londoners added Monday to their weekend, a tradition of skiving that it took a world war to stop. Craft workers would spend the day down the pub or visiting distant friends by that new-fangled invention, the steam engine. But in the 20th century, the relaxed world of the craft worker no longer exists; weavers and bakers have been replaced by bankers and accountants, and there's no room for slacking off.

There *are* companies, however, that do things differently. At the large end of the scale is **WL Gore**, the textile manufacturer that may have kept you dry on your bike ride to work. Gore opened its first international offices in London in 1964 and now has a turnover of more than £1.5 billion – so it's clearly doing something right. But for such a massive enterprise, there's an astonishing and deep-rooted radicalism to the company. There are no bosses, just leaders. Associates (employees) choose to follow leaders, who work on one or two projects at a time. The evidence seems to be that this improves innovation – the company has brought out long-life guitar strings and breathable bagpipes as a result. 'Dabbling' – devoting 10 per cent of your time to your own schemes – is encouraged. 'Gore is not the place for people driven by status or career path,' says would-be CEO John Housego. The four principles enshrined by founder Bill Gore are freedom, commitment, fairness and waterline (how to decide how big a risk to take). Note the absence of the words 'growth' and 'profit' – although the family firm is thought to have made a profit every year of its existence. The employees thrive on responsibility and independence, which translates to low staff turnover and high employee satisfaction.

Satisfaction was at the heart of how the three founders of London-based drinks company, **Innocent**, saw their young business. Now based at Fruit Towers in Shepherds Bush, the smoothie producers whizzed up their first batch of fruit at a London music festival and asked customers to vote 'yes' or 'no'. Ten years later, Innocent employs 300 people and has its own London music festival, Fruitstock. In that time they've developed some distinctly slow strategies for keeping their employees happy at the successful, not-so-little company.

'It's the dumb but important things you do that make a difference,' says Dan Germain, Creative Director. 'Providing a breakfast is one of the most effective: in London many people skip breakfast or just charge up with a coffee. But starting the day with proper food makes people ready to go. And there's a club for everything: climbing, cycling, even cheese – we have a lot of people who love cheese. We provide an allowance for starting any club. Once a week we have masseurs come in and we get interesting people to talk to us about how to manage stress. And we have plenty of space in which to think as well as work. We're open to whatever people suggest.'

Dan has worked with Innocent from the outset and had the rare opportunity to help shape the place. 'We asked ourselves: what if we could do this or that? What things would we most like to provide people? We had certain goals, like creating a company culture and getting people to get to know each other so it becomes familial. We considered doing conventional team-building days, where you build a raft together, but there are cuter, nicer ways of doing that. Every year we have a company weekend away – the first year it was snowboarding for just six people, the next year it was 12 people, then 30. Last year we took 300 people to Spain.

'Now that we're 300 employees, maybe we're slowing down as a business but we've kept it as we wanted it. There are plenty of people who have worked here for a while and what they do goes far beyond the call of duty. You can have all the table football machines in the world but if you have people who aren't inspired you'll go nowhere.'

But the process of starting a company is far from laidback and it's only recently that Dan has been able to downshift to four days a week. 'I used to work incredibly long hours,' he says. 'I'd arrive at work at 7am and rarely leave before 7 or 8pm. But I was young, had energy and the company was growing. These days I will get to work early but leave early. You can do most days' work in four or five hours if you're smart.

'My wife would tell you that I still need to sort out my work-life balance. There have definitely been times when I've had to tell myself that it's only a job, that it's only fruit juice and that the most important people are friends and family.'

As with many London workers, Dan found that getting exercise during the day helped – not in a sterile, windowless gym, but out-doors. 'My thing is running. I found that running before work helped; the serotonins made me work better and it helps you get back in touch with your body, reminds you that you're flesh and blood, not an exten-sion to a computer. There's a weird rhythm to running and it seems to help me come up with different words and patterns. Your mind wanders. Even driving is a slight liberation. If I've been for a run and have a shower after-wards, I spend the last three or four minutes just feeling the warm water on my head. There's always something keeping you from those moments of meditation – a phone, a lap-top, a meeting. But not in the shower.' The slower pace of life has even reached Dan's home: 'I was surprised one year to find myself enjoying gardening. I have a two-year-old who loves painting and drawing so I have also rediscovered arts and crafts.'

As Dan has learned, it is the human ele-ment that matters most in any company, whether it makes waterproofs or smoothies. He explains: 'You don't think you'll need to be managing people, when that's actually the most difficult thing: keeping them happy, growing personally and motivated.' 🐎

BE

SLOW DOWN AND SMELL THE ROSES

SEE

HEAR

SMELL

TASTE

TOUCH

see

SITES FOR SORE EYES

"

WHAT YOU SEE IS WHAT YOU GET.

Traditional

"

Sight is our most over stimulated sense, and in London we're swamped with unreal images – advertising, marketing, spin – vying for our attention and trying to convince us things are what they're not. Sure, we've got our eyes open but are we actually still seeing? When we really look, we can see wonder in the mundane. We notice how the light illuminates City buildings differently at various times of year; stop, look up and stare and we might appreciate anew the craftsmanship of Sir Christopher Wren; spot a piece of graffiti that sums up how we feel; or notice colours change in the garden.

Cut through the dross to see how things really are, literally through nature, and laterally through art. Or imagine it's 20 years hence and you're asked to describe in vivid detail London circa 2010. What would it look like? If how we see the world is shaped by our own personality and expectations, we only need alter that perception and the whole world will change with us.

Looking Back

Culture and history abound in a city as old and labyrinthine as ours. Local oddities act like viewfinders, focusing our gaze on the details to help us see London more clearly. Likewise, stories are scattered around our streets, homes and museums, rewarding the curious with a view into the city's past and how it has shaped our character.

EYES PEELED The best view of **Battersea Power Station** is from the northern riverbank at sunset. There's an endearing fragility to the structure: semi-derelict walls propping up such assured chimneys, proudly lording over the slow-flowing Thames. Besides its imposing, industrial beauty, the real wonder of the thing is that it's still standing. It has languished without a roof, the steel frame exposed to the elements, since 1989 when construction of a theme park was abandoned due to escalating costs. The silent, stubborn giant, a monument to our industrial heritage, clearly didn't fancy such desecration. All sorts of developments have been proposed since it stopped generating power in 1983, although frankly we're wondering if they'll ever come off. We wouldn't mind if it mimicked its cousin, the Bankside Power Station, restored and revitalised and now the heart of contemporary culture as the **Tate Modern**. Sir Giles Gilbert Scott designed both buildings, although he's perhaps more fondly remembered for the darling red telephone boxes dotted around the city like unemployed gnomes in a garden. Thanks to mobile phones, the K6 – as it's known in the industry – is on the outer and BT is looking for ideas on what to do with them.

It's easy to take our poor old river crossings for granted, or even curse their bottlenecking tendencies as we rush about on the daily commute. But a wander over **Albert Bridge** can cure all that. With its ornate lanterns and pastel pagodas, it must be the prettiest (if most endangered) bridge in town, greeted on either side by the lush embankments of Chelsea and Battersea Park. Who can resist a smile at the curious notice, 'All troops must break step when marching over this bridge'? Nearby Chelsea Barracks feared The Trembling Lady wouldn't withstand their weight as they paraded home from training and battle. Be mindful of every step on the weathered deck as you cross, listening for the echoes of forgotten footfall, your hand running along the cool iron railings to steady you in the present.

On the greengrocer's shelf the humble **pineapple** doesn't raise an eyebrow. But bracketing Lambeth Bridge it becomes a link to an 18th-century world where the pineapple was a status symbol and most effective way of telling the world that you'd arrived. Each one cost the equivalent of £5000, but within a century 200,000 were being unloaded each year at London's docks and the fad was over. But not before the fruit had left its mark on railings from Kensington and Mayfair to Soho Square and Whitehall.

A PRIVILEGED VIEW OF BATTERSEA POWER STATION, PEERING IN FROM THE BASE OF THE SOUTHWEST CHIMNEY

There are Pineapple pubs, pineapples in iron and stone, pineapples on top of the National Gallery and St Paul's Cathedral, and in Kew Gardens (to name a few).

Lampposts illuminate the city's past, from the Embankment's magnificent globe-bearing examples to the galleons on top of those at Admiralty Arch and the Sherlock Holmes lamp outside the Ship and Shovel pub on Craven Passage. Some were gas-powered, others electric, and there are even a few left with the metal hooks for whale blubber. But in Carting Lane, off the Strand, one particular lamp has the cartoon illumination of a great idea. A Webb Patent Sewer Gas Lamp known as **'Iron Lilly'**, it is fuelled by air drawn from the sewers beneath, preventing a build-up of odours and gas in the sewer system (it wasn't for nothing that Carting Lane became known to locals as 'farting lane'). It has been alight day and night since the 19th century, apparently, save for a short injury break after a run-in with a lorry.

MUSEUMS In 2009 a giant cocoon appeared in the **Natural History Museum** (*Cromwell Rd; www.nhm. ac.uk*), to celebrate the 200th anniversary of Charles Darwin's birth. The eight-storey creation houses 17 million insects and some of the museum's 220 scientific staff, hard at work and, like the dead specimens, classified by type: botanists, butterfly experts and beetle boffins side by side. Peer over Jan Beccaloni's shoulder – she's the Curator of Arachnids – or ask her husband George, Curator of Cockroaches, what he's working on. According to Director of Science Richard Lane, the new building represents the museum's transition from an introverted space to an extrovert place, helping to communicate a sense of wonder at the natural world.

Wandering from the Greek-inspired pillars of the façade to the sunlit glass of Norman Foster's Great Court and through the halls of ancient artefacts, the **British Museum** (*Great Russell St; www.britishmuseum.org*) is a place to connect with a longer sense of humanity, and to contemplate tradition, culture and the passage of time. The museum itself was founded around the Enlightenment idea that, despite their differences, human cultures can understand one another through mutual engagement. Consider the souls who wielded those stone tools or wound that 16th-century watch, and then ponder the contribution of our own era – a 3.5m-high artwork using decommissioned weapons from Mozambique's recent Civil War, turning the threat they posed into a textured sculpture of rusted metal branches and birds' nests, aptly titled the *Tree of Life*.

Rather more eclectic, Frederick Horniman represents the greatest influence on London: trade. The 19th-century tea-trader was an avid collector and trawled the world to bring back specimens now housed at the **Horniman Museum** (*100 London Rd, Forest Hill; 020 8699 1872; www.horniman.ac.uk*). A 17th-century French horn sits alongside a charming WWI jazz drum kit, Qing dynasty jewels and rare fossils from around the world. Compact gardens engage all the senses with plots of indigenous plants from all over the world while a marvellous Victorian conservatory stages world music concerts in summer. The entire space invites us to contemplate the threads that bind London to India, Africa and Britain's other former colonies, and what those places have brought to London.

HOUSES Poets, scientists, dukes and philosophers all made London home, and their houses provide intimate portals into their lives and loves. No wonder English Heritage is so keen to share the stories and scatter blue plaques all over town, or that we scramble to uncover architectural secrets when the **Open House festival** (*www. openhouse.org.uk*) unlocks some 700 doors to the public each autumn.

Our favourite house belongs to a fictitious family; humble Huguenot silk-weavers in Spitalfields, a long-time creative corner of the capital. Their 19th-century home was created by Dennis Severs, an American artist who lived in the house at 18 Folgate St in the 1960s and 1970s. **Dennis Severs' House** *(020 7247 4013; www.dennissevershouse. co.uk)* is open every Monday evening and lit by candlelight. Affecting all the senses, it prompts thoughts of reason, passion and harmony, and how we balance those against the grind of life. The house's rooms are as if someone has just left by another door. Sounds and smells linger in the air, while indulgences strewn around the rooms depict the *joie de vivre* of the weavers.

Down House *(Luxted Rd, Downe; 01689 859 119; www.english-heritage.org.uk)*, on the outskirts of London, offers a more prag-matic kind of slowness. It's clear that Charles Darwin wasn't one to rush things, and he spent years at home here letting his ideas percolate. He pondered natural selection and the ape skull on his desk from the comfort of his faded black armchair or strolled in the garden, what he called his 'outdoor laboratory'. Darwin proved that by taking notice of the little things, in his case the worms in the garden, we get to understand greater truths. The earthworms may have benefited too: Darwin would ask his family to serenade them. 'From so simple a beginning,' he wrote, 'endless forms most beautiful and most wonderful have been, and are being, evolved.'

Hampstead was home to **John Keats** *(Keats Grove; 020 7435 2062; www.cityoflondon. gov.uk)* and his sensory garden inspired him to pen, among other things, *Ode to a Nightingale*. But the neighbourhood's literary inspiration doesn't end there, and we're fond of 2 Willow Rd, a rare and beautiful example of Modernism in the city *(020 7435 6166; www.nationaltrust.org.uk)*, designed by **Erno Goldfinger** in 1939. His neighbour, Ian Fleming, was so infuriated by the demolition of the original Victorian properties that he named a Bond villain after the architect who went on design some of the most hideous tower blocks of the 1970s.

Colours of London

There's regal **red**, **black** cabs and **grey** gravitas but London is expanding its palette. There's **white** for the Shri Swaminarayan Mandir temple in Neasden, the largest Hindu temple outside India, and countless shades of **green** for our new environmentalism. But perhaps London's heart is **gold**, representing love with the Albert Memorial in Hyde Park, law with the Statue of Justice on top of the Old Bailey and money, keeping the wheels of the City turning.

LOOKING TO THE FUTURE AT THE OPEN HOUSE FESTIVAL

Painting the Town

London is a city of magnificent views; of wide dramatic skies, hilltop panoramas, daring architecture, ancient trees and wonderful bridges. Not that we locals get to see that often, scurrying about with our blinkers on or power-walking across Blackfriars Bridge with a blank gaze. Even tourists, snapping at famous buildings, are not actually looking at the city. Digital cameras have eliminated the need to scrutinise a view before attempting to capture it, and a successful picture is now a matter of chance, rather than eye.

John Ruskin, himself raised in the smart London suburb of Herne Hill, insists in *The Elements of Drawing* that by learning to draw a man 'may ensure his seeing truly'. Before cameras, if one wanted to preserve the memory of a view or beautiful thing, one would whip out one's sketchbook, pencil and watercolours and spend an hour or more in the business of recording it. And after so much time and effort had been spent in the recreation of a scene, how could it ever be forgotten? With this in mind, let's do away with our cameras and their shortcuts, and instead try to see London properly by drawing it.

Whenever I have an afternoon to spare I pack my sketchbook and go hunting for things to draw. I find a perch, a low wall or bench, and give myself a few hours, seeing something new every time I lift my head to remind myself of what I am actually trying to render.

Favourites, so far, are the views down from Gipsy Hill to the centre of town – among the modern buildings, wheels and gherkins, St Paul's Cathedral is still the most striking form, just as it would have been 200 years ago when gipsies stalked this area. The elegant lines of Sir John Soane's Dulwich Picture Gallery are also very pleasing to try and recreate, offering an almost mathematical problem. An attempt at the Houses of Parliament illustrates just how intricate and complicated neo-Gothic architecture can be. Albert Bridge, with its pastel flourishes and delicate suspension, is an excellent subject and also gives one the chance to have a go at the grey menace of the Thames and the sublimity of London's ever changing skies.

Just as London transforms under the gaze of the artist, its colours becoming brighter and its lines more graceful, so time is different when you are drawing. In fact, in my experience, it seems to stop altogether. So much focus is required to draw something, to hold it in the head and recreate it on paper, even not very well, that hours can tick by unnoticed; the only indication that lunch has become afternoon is that the shadows are falling differently and the colours have become softer.

It is a practice like no other, allowing the head to become empty of all thought, blocking out noise and other urban botheration. It is the nearest I get to meditation (but be warned, people *will* peer over your shoulder and ask what you are doing).

PAINTING THE THAMES NEAR GABRIEL'S WHARF

Of course, I am by no means the first to appreciate London in this way. Hogarth showed the seamier side of the city and Turner is famous for his views of the Thames, later inspiring Monet. My neighbourhood artist, Camille Pissarro, lived in Upper Norwood during the Franco-Prussian war and painted many local scenes. My favourite is of Fox Hill, a winding street five minutes from my house, which Pissarro painted on a frosty winter day, snow on the pavements, grey smoke billowing from a chimney pot and the black trees bare. I have managed to locate the spot from which he worked and make my own version; not only does this give me an insight into Pissarro's technique (Ruskin is very big on the benefits of copying superior artists) but it also shows me how much London has transformed in the intervening years.

Some artists' depictions of London are harder to follow. Canaletto, high on his fame as the master-painter of Venice, came to London in 1746 and painted numerous scenes, most strikingly one using an arch of Westminster Bridge as a half-tondo frame. But his juxtapositions are sometimes imaginary and his perspectives often impossible to recreate. In a Canaletto painting the sky is always a sparkling blue and the water glints gold with a warm sun, whether it is London or Venice.

Whistler, on the other hand, though he might be deemed the truest painter of London, with his streets so blurry with smog that the only perceptible feature is a smudge of orange denoting a lit window, drew a series of wonderful lithographs of the Thames from the window of his rooms on the sixth floor of the Savoy Hotel. Sadly the vantage point would cost rather a lot for the modern artist to assume. But it doesn't matter, for there are myriad beautiful and interesting compositions to be found all over London, from Parliament Hill to Crystal Palace. All you need are a bit of time, paper, a pencil and the spirit of Ruskin urging you on: 'If you wish to obtain quicker perceptions of the beauty of the natural world, and to preserve something like a true image of beautiful things that pass away, or which you must yourself leave… then I can help you.' ᛭

Gavanndra Hodge

Art and Soul

Art, like nature, has the power to take us out of ourselves, to inspire our thoughts and console us at times of personal need. Profoundly important in such a hectic city, art gives us a lateral way of seeing through the clutter to what's really going on.

GALLERIES 'Paintings emit a stillness and silence,' writes Justin Paton in *How to Look at a Painting*. 'It's where small things become large, dead people look you in the eye, and a bubble trembles on the brink of bursting for 270 years. And so, in good hands, it is still one of the best ways we have for looking at the world afresh.'

With so many masterpieces to choose from, it's tempting to join the crowds and seek out nothing else. But art should be a tonic rather than a binge, a fillip to the working day rather than a chin-stroker's charter. There's no ticket for soaking it in, no clock, no suggested duration. In recent years we've been blessed with free entry to great galleries, affording afternoon interludes as often as we like.

Slow icon Carl Honoré agrees: 'I very often pop into the National Portrait Gallery or the Wallace Collection and I just go to see one painting and stay there about 10 minutes and then go. I find that very recharging. Something about a real work of art is very slowing and you develop a relationship over time with certain paintings. It's like having a friend.'

Blockbuster exhibitions offer too much for the observer to absorb, reckons art critic Laura Cumming. Far better, she says, for an artwork to be given a room of its own, as Titian's *Diana and Actaeon* was at the National Gallery in 2008, allowing you to take in the work at your own pace, let your eye absorb its minute details and wait for it to unfold before you.

Let us linger in the **National Gallery** *(Trafalgar Square; www.nationalgallery.org.uk)* a little longer, with this smugly subjective smattering of slow-minded paintings – vigorous disagreement is welcome, chin-scratching optional. Titian exemplifies a slow approach to art; his *Bacchus* and *Ariadne* captures love, passion and the infinite possibilities of a new day. Let yourself sink into the deep blue, starry sky and feel the excitement in the sunrise.

There's something deeply meditative about the muted colours the Dutch and Flemish masters used in their portraits. In Room 25 of the National Gallery allow Vermeer take you away from the hurly burly, or immerse yourself in the steady gaze of Rembrandt's *Self Portrait* in the dun-coloured Swinstead Van Walsem room. The painting is a moving, affirming reminder of the passage of time.

The dying days of a distinguished warship as it is towed up the Thames to the breakers' yard at Rotherhithe are evoked by Turner's *The Fighting Temeraire*. The painting, one of the great depictions of the capital, shows steam technology supplanting sail against a smoky, hazy sunset over 19th century London. It reminds us that the city is always in flux and that there's beauty amid its industry. Turner's talent was in capturing nature's moods and the effect of sunlight, rain, fog and storms upon it.

see...

ART STORM, TATE MODERN

MODERN ART Galleries open and close in a weekend and instant 'pop-up' shows, publicised by Facebook, Twitter and word of mouth, mean London's contemporary arts scene is fragmented and often ephemeral but always gathering pace. The East End is still pockmarked with galleries but the energy is slowly crossing the river, lured by the annual **Deptford X Art Festival** and the **Bearspace Gallery** *(152 Deptford High St; 020 8694 8097; www.bearspace.co.uk)*. All over London, communities spring up from art schools, studios, galleries and postcodes, nurturing emerging talent and bringing creative souls together.

The **Horse Hospital** *(Colonnade; 020 7833 3644; www.thehorsehospital.com)* in Bloomsbury is the spiritual home of avant-garde art, film, fashion and music in London. A step closer to the establishment lies the **Institute of Contemporary Arts** *(The Mall; 020 7930 3647; www.ica.org.uk)*, a haven for the offbeat and experimental that delights in polarising opinions. The beautiful Georgian building, regally situated between Trafalgar Square and Buckingham Palace, belies the radicalism adorning the whitewashed walls within, the contrast making for a lovely slow day of strolling and art appreciation. They'll also point you towards some of the best **artist-run spaces** around town – galleries and grassroots initiatives run by artists, for artists, that thumb their noses at commerce (for a while at least) and focus on innovation and experimentation. This youthful force reminds us of art's raw energy, driven by expression, inviting us to connect at an instinctive level rather than with concern for renown or critique.

PUBLIC ART In comparison to the static statements of London's historic statues, the shifting displays on Trafalgar's Square's **Fourth Plinth** *(www.fourthplinth.co.uk)* capture the restless spirit of today and reflect a desire to engage the city and its inhabitants. They're evidence that we no longer define ourselves by our military accomplishments, but rather by myriad subtle factors, not least our creativity and individuality.

Elsewhere around town, our favourite pieces of public whimsy – partly favourite because rather than shouting 'look at me' they lie waiting to be discovered – include *Paddington Bear*, with a corner to himself in Paddington Station and *Peter Pan* in Kensington Gardens. The *Girl with Dolphin* near Tower Bridge seems tragically distant from the *Boy with Dolphin* by Albert Bridge, which seems to defy gravity in order to play.

CINEMA Just off Leicester Square, the **Prince Charles Cinema** *(Leicester Pl; www.princecharlescinema.com)* sticks it to the anodyne West End megaplexes. At times a struggling theatre and pornographic filmhouse, the Prince Charles is now deservedly one of the city's favourite independent cinemas.

Of course, all that really matters is who you're sharing your popcorn with, so try score one of the couches at the back of the **Electric Cinema** *(191 Portobello Rd; www.electriccinema.co.uk)*. More like a pack of retro Love Hearts, the **Coronet** *(103 Notting Hill Gate; www.coronet.org)* is a timeworn classic, and with the air of a proper old-school tiered theatre, it's one of most soulful places to catch an arthouse film.

Combine architecture with cinema at East Finchley's art deco **Phoenix Cinema** *(52 High Road; www.phoenixcinema.co.uk)* or the **Ritzy** *(Coldharbour Lane, Brixton; www.picturehouses.co.uk)*, which, despite its make-overs, retains its ramshackle Edwardian charm (indulge in a blockbuster for a gander around stately Screen One). Meanwhile, the long-derelict art deco **Hoxton Cinema** in Pitfield St has been earmarked for rejuvenation for so long now we're wondering if it'll ever happen. The projectors were switched off in 1956, but the neon sign has ensured its status as a local icon and a tribute to enduring independent spirit.

What **BFI** *(Belvedere Rd, South Bank; www.bfi.org.uk)* lacks in charm, it makes up for in certain quality, as the spiritual home of British filmmakers past and present, poking and prodding the local consciousness and keeping it reel.

THEATRE From centuries-old theatres to drama in the park, London has a unique affinity with the stage, a place for expression and contemplation, which invites us to engage in a way the screen can't. 'The theatre is much more than a place to witness a play,' explains local playwright Luke Redmond. 'It is a place to inspire and to be inspired; a place to see, hear, feel and think. You could say London itself is a theatre, catering for every taste, and every sense, every mind and every soul.

'Shakespeare's wooden "O" seems to hold the energy and echo the applause of the last 400 years. A stone's throw from the Globe is the (relatively contemporary) National Theatre and the Olivier, an unbelievable fusion of engineering and design. Yet for all its pow-erful pullies and colossal cogs, the space is as smooth as any ballet, as musical as any opera, and as dramatic as any one of the great plays that have resounded in its mighty space.'

Slow even crosses the Thames to Theatreland – really! – if you choose to connect meaningfully with its culture and commentary. 'Though commercially rammed,' Luke tells us, 'the West End is packed with drama, comedy, morality and pathos. It's simply keeping with the times, expanding and evolving as every business must. Keep in mind, even Shakespeare was contemporary in his day.

'Resonating in every direction, there lies a myriad of smaller theatres, tiny 30-seaters, little lofts and cellars. The fringe network is a vibrant and energetic web spun across the entire city. Many venues, like the Battersea Arts Centre, are crucial cultural hubs where the whole neighbourhood comes together to share stories and experiences.

'The world-famous Royal Court – just like the Soho Theatre, the Tricycle, the Old Vic – has long provided support and opportunity for new playwrights,' says Luke. 'Shakespeare and Marlowe provoked a debate between church and art that raged for centuries; later, George Bernard Shaw and Samuel Beckett helped us rediscover why theatre is important, reflecting as it does on the lives we live. John Osborne inspired a movement of Angry Young Men, riling the establishment to such an extent that popular culture hasn't looked the same since. Thousands of writers have their place within the drama of this city. Theatre and London are symbiotic: they help each other to live and breathe. The theatre provides the essential outpouring of new ideas and new energy.'

The City as a Canvas

Street art aficionado Ed Bartlett explains where to look and why.

I spent last Friday circling London in search of Adam Neate. Well, not Neate himself, but one of the 1000 original artworks he had secreted about the city as gifts for lucky passers-by. Not surprisingly, given that examples of his work now sell for thousands of pounds, I wasn't the only person on the hunt.

With a vast, diverse population, a unique energy and the concentration of creative industries, it's no wonder London is at the epicentre of the world's street art movement. Most interesting is the relationship between all these factors – the shifting borders between rich and poor, decay and gentrification, branded and unbranded, all played out 24 hours a day on the streets of London. This provides the rich vein of socio-political material that is the key to great street art.

You can see street art anywhere: much of its impact comes from stumbling upon a new piece where or when you least expect it. The most famous hotspot is the tunnel on Leake St, two minutes stroll from the London Eye. This disused service road beneath Waterloo station was transformed in May 2008 by Banksy and other street artists from around the world into a three-day urban art extravaganza dubbed the Cans Festival. Such was the event's popularity that the site has become a living gallery.

Beyond that, Hoxton, Shoreditch and Hackney offer the best street art in the capital. Last Friday's wanderings took me around the 'golden triangle' of Great Eastern St, Shoreditch High St and Old St to get my bearings before diving off into side streets such as Paul St, Blackall St, Willow St, Curtain Rd and Rivington St to experience a dizzying array of creative styles and cultural (and sometimes political) messages. Bringing it indoors, there are some great specialist galleries such as Pictures on Walls (www.picturesonwalls.com), Pure Evil (www.pureevil.eu) and Black Rat Press (www.blackratpress.co.uk).

One of the exciting things about street art is that you don't need to be an established name to get your works on the walls. There are no sniffy curators hanging around the back streets of Hackney deciding who 'gets up'. For those willing to face the consequences of getting caught (for better or worse, it is illegal), it's possible to build a significant international following in a fraction of the time it would take a traditionally schooled artist to do so. Besides Banksy and Adam Neate, some of the hottest works to look out for include the retro videogame mosaics of Invader, the giant stylised typography of Eine, the comic book superheroes of Cept and the colourful toothy grins of Sweet Toof. You are just as likely to see international artists, from Brooklyn-based collective Faile, through to the gigantic photographic paste-ups of JR to the surreal Python-esque neon collages of Judith Supine.

But did I find an Adam Neate? No, and it didn't spoil the adventure one bit. ✦

Ed Bartlett

hear

LISTEN TO LONDON

> **DON'T UNDERESTIMATE THE VALUE OF DOING NOTHING, OF JUST GOING ALONG, LISTENING TO ALL THE THINGS YOU CAN'T HEAR, AND NOT BOTHERING.**
> Winnie the Pooh

They say cockneys are born within earshot of Bow's bells, and Londoners from Dick Whittington to Samuel Pepys have heard St Mary-le-Bow's peals. But what chance would they have these days amid the clamour of engines, sirens, shouting and the incessant beeping of our own bloody gadgets? Noise and speed seem intimately entwined, and the faster we get the louder our impatience and desperation.

But beneath the hubbub lies a more subtle soundscape, distinct rhythms and riffs that distinguish London from anywhere else on the planet, day from night, one season from another, even one street to the next. Certain sounds are heard only here – 'mind the gap' – while others, such as the song of a lark or nightingale (no longer, alas, in Berkeley Square) are an invisible link to a natural world beyond the bricks and mortar.

Rhythms, Riffs and Recordings

A melancholy cellist busks on the South Bank, her heart-wrenching trill competing with the sizzle from a hotdog stand nearby. Spray cans rattle in an underpass at Waterloo, as monastic plainsong echoes solemnly from above, a failed deterrent. A bongo drummer provides rhythm to a drunken West End street – a musical comedy, perhaps? Blackbirds serenade suburban rooftops against the din of traffic below, while insects fizz behind a football match at Hackney Marshes. Ambling through Ian Rawes' aural archive of London, it becomes clear that he is not merely recording sound. He's recording the mood of the city across fragments in time: its residents – every race, every class, every species, – their hopes and conflicts, habits and beliefs.

'I thought about taking photos, but I'm hopeless at that,' chuckles Ian, a born and bred Londoner who's taken it upon himself to collect the city's sounds, organising and archiving them as the grassroots London Sound Survey *(www.soundsurvey.org.uk)*. 'It seemed interesting to document the place you grew up in. In a small way you've borne witness to it. I don't mean a celebration – I'm quite ambivalent about living in London personally – but a real documentation, for better or for worse. The city is a kind of vortex that draws from the energy of the young people who come to live and work in it, but for me, middle-aged, I'm just living here. I'm trying to make sense of the city, understand it, connect with it.'

Sounds can represent fashions, 'from singing canaries and wind chimes to boom-boxes and car horns that play the first eight notes of "Colonel Bogey"'. They reflect developments in trade, industry and technology; growth of the city itself; demographic and social change; even shifts in the scattering of wildlife, like the raspy squawk of the ring-necked parakeet as it becomes astonishingly prevalent here. There are two categories of sound, Ian tells us: incidental sounds, 'like traffic, industry, footsteps, a yawn or cough', and those made to serve a function, 'things like the cries of street market traders, church bells, announcements that the train's running late, and animals – they don't make their sounds for us, but they are just as deliberate'.

We start with silence: calming, contemplative – and practically non-existent, according to the sound collector. 'Traffic, birdsong and aeroplane noise, depending on flight paths, are the three constant sounds in London. Even if you seek out remote wooded areas, on the outskirts of the city, you'll still hear traffic during the day; it might be dimmer but you can't get away from it.' The constant hum seems to close the city in; our ears tune into the sounds in our own neighbourhood, rather than those across town. Ian illustrates the point: 'You have to be quite close to Big Ben to actually hear it chime. In past days you'd hear it further because there was less background din. Samuel Pepys used to hear the bells of Barking, from where he lived out near St Paul's! You'd never hear that now.'

As Ian points out, birdsong melts the most urbanised hearts. 'The blackbird has a beautiful song. Everybody should get up at least once to experience the dawn chorus. Even right in the centre of town, like at St James' Park, you can hear birdsong.' On that note, he's posted a delightful recording, kicked off by ducks and geese, their deep, languid coos enticing chirpy chatter between increasing numbers of other species. Their voices herald dawn, confirmed by six background, on-the-hour gongs from Big Ben.

Sounds can connect us intimately to time and place, and drench our memories. 'I was brought up in central London,' says Ian, 'and I used to go to Berwick Street Market with my mother, it was much bigger and louder then. I still love the costermongers with their cries all over the city; they tend to be outgoing people, full of character. At a supermarket, the only excitement is when they move your corn flakes from aisle 11 to aisle 2.' He's recorded the cockney cries at the Columbia Road Flower Market ('Cheap enough to give to somebody you don't like!') and the abrasive hawking of cheapjack traders at East Street ('Not £29.99, not ten pound, but a fiver!'). 'If you read old books – right back to people like Henry Mayhew – the market traders' cries haven't changed that much, so they're part of the city's cultural traditions.'

Ian's recordings capture song at every turn: buskers, drunks, melodies escaping from shops and bars. 'I'm always quite intrigued at song,' he explains. 'Song is something a lot of people pay to see, but don't do much of themselves anymore. There are a couple of pubs where people still sing and play around a piano but DIY music is a bit of a cliché

now. People used to sell sheet music in the streets, there was a culture of having a song together. Whistling is the same, you used to hear it everywhere, all the workers. You'd see little signs on posh hotels saying the tradesmen must not whistle. There's less of it now; popular music has moved away from melody towards rhythm, so it's harder to whistle.

'But I don't think you can be nostalgic about those sorts of things,' he insists. 'One has to be oriented on the present and find things to appreciate now. You can't recreate the past and if you try, you end up somewhere really different. Historical study asks how we got here, how we got to the state we're in, but nostalgia is about mulling.'

He's stumped when asked about individual voices of London. 'So many people come and go in a place like this, and to single them out becomes a bit forced.' He ponders. 'There used to be a very funny old guy at London Bridge, he'd always announce the trains by saying, "When you feel the wind blowing…" You know, that in itself is a curious sound, that deep hollow rumbling. As a little kid it was terrifying, like a monster coming out of a cave. It's a great sound, I haven't recorded that one yet…" As the sound collector muses, I can hear his weekend plans unfolding. What better way to mark time? 🐎

Hayley Cull

Schedule of Sound

Forget seeing in the New Year on 1 **January**; *hear* it in with the cascading chimes of Big Ben and set off on your year of living aurally. The *Westminster Quarters* – that contemplative E Major melody played to mark the time – brings the festive chatter to a frosty hush, clearing the sky before 12 great solemn gongs give way to the popping of champagne corks and a wave of new beginnings.

Should you lose your way later in the year, seek out bells and let their uncomplicated peals bring you back to this clear moment, when the fresh opportunities are laid out ahead; you can even ring them yourself at churches such as St Dunstan's in Stepney, St James's in Bermondsey and St Mary's in Barnes (ring *them* first).

Air molecules huddle closer together on cold days, so sound travels faster and further. Perhaps this is why the honks of geese in parklands seem ever louder on a chilly **February** morning, joined by the crackling of coots and the coos and caws of gulls, all chatting merrily. If you need convincing, check out the London Wetland Centre *(Queen Elizabeth Walk)*.

Meanwhile, the human chorus lyricises our own community, the most linguistically diverse place on earth with more than 250 languages spoken. Mellifluous Russian, Tamil, Farsi and Somali meet varied English dialects, entwining with the music and cultural patter they each bring to the streets. Chinatown makes the point with a bang, ringing in the Chinese New Year with firecrackers and lion dances.

As the sun rises higher in the sky in **March**, birds begin their mating songs. Listen to the rise and fall of a lark singing, loitering in uncultivated greenery like Wormwood Scrubs or Hampstead Heath. The tiny speck in the sky seems to stop time with its song: 'Like a poet / Hidden in the light of thought,' wrote Shelley. As chicks fledge and venture from the nest, diligent parents call to them; the relationship is as dependent on sound as much as vision.

Spring Equinox brings World Storytelling Day *(www.freewebs.com/worldstorytellingday)*, where fanciful tales fall on eager ears all over the world. Oral storytelling is the oldest art form of all, reminds Ben Haggarty, founder of the Crick Crack Club *(www.crickcrackclub. com)*, the longstanding outlet for London storytellers. 'One of the reasons people are drawn to these big brushstrokes of emotion is that it takes them out of their comfort zone.' Tune into local events or start your own.

Sporadic showers in **April** hammer away at our premature summer optimism. Listen to the sound the rain makes on different surfaces: bursting on city streets, pattering on the stretched fabric of umbrellas, or splashing into the rivers, themselves rasping under the downpour. Nothing flushes city-addled minds clear like a good soaking.

Warm **May** bring a new buzz, the lazy drone of bumblebees working their way between flowers. According to the Bumblebee Conservation Trust *(www.bumblebeeconservation.org.uk)*, it's a sound on the wane as front gardens become driveways and electromagnetic interference affects their navigation (although Orlando Clarke tells a different story of his Brixton honeybees, p113). Bumblebees themselves have no ears, feeling sound in vibrations.

The long days of **June** are packed with outdoor attractions, most enchanting of which can be listening to music while surrounded by nature. A final flourish is added as the sun sets behind stately properties, like Kenwood House for the Picnic Concerts and Music On A Summer Evening, and Somerset House for the popular Summer Series.

This time of year is about 'new balls please' and the hush of Wimbledon's Centre Court – at times perhaps the quietest place in London – occasionally broken by the novelty ring of some plonker's mobile. Cricket grounds hum to the rhythmic thwack of leather on willow and excited shouts of 'Howzat!' Laughter peals over grassy commons as families emerge from who-knows-where to kick a ball. The chimes of ice-cream vans whip us back to sprinkle-coated summers.

Even the rude awakening from a car alarm can be a blessing if it gets you up in time for the dawn chorus in **July**. Swifts and house martins are the most elegant signs summer has arrived, arcing across the skies after insects with shrill screams and whistles, and darting and diving over ponds at West Croydon and Thornton Heath. Flies can be heard buzzing above the water in the warm weather, luring fish to the surface for a snack. It all happens so fast that the splash back down might be the first you know of it.

Meanwhile, London's bats feed over the lakes of Hampstead Heath and Kew Gardens, stalked by their own battarazi (amateur bat-spotters). Kenwood House issues very technically titled 'magic black boxes', which translate their inaudible squeaks into sound we can hear.

When the swifts have left for Africa and the bats are readying for winter hibernation, the wild chorus moves to football grounds in **August** and the start of the new season when the stands are in full throat, and fans are

Busking

Unexpected melodies can stop us in our tracks, clearing mind and lifting moods. Buskers enhance our sonic landscape (well, some of them) and you never know what you'll come across; a lone guitarist on a street corner, a band of steel drummers in the South Bank's underpasses, or an internationally renowned concert violinist on her Stradivarius . A couple of years ago, at the invitation of *The Independent*, violinist Tamsin Little busked under Waterloo Bridge. In 45 minutes, more than a thousand people passed by, eight stopped to listen and just £14.10 hit her case. 'Sometimes we're guilty of giving ourselves a goal, even if it's only catching a train,' she later reflected of the concert crowds hurrying by, 'leaving very little room for spontaneity in our lives.'

roused by old chants and entertained by new ditties ('Let's all go to Tesco's, where Millwall get their best clothes').

But it's not just footballers going head-to-head in autumn; you can also hear the positively frenzied sound of fallow deer bucks and red stags rutting in Richmond Park, Bushy Park and the Deer Park at Greenwich. Shocking, primal roars accompany the stamping of hooves and the crisp, fencing clash of antlers. Seeing the uninterested female – the purpose of all this ruckus in the first place – blissfully unaware, enjoying a patch of grass, turns this aural action movie into an overblown romantic comedy.

Days darken under **September** shadows, and we get the occasional thunderstorm. Word goes out on the increasingly hysterical bird telegraph, hushing in an electrified moment of stillness before the skies break. From the safety of a good window, enjoy the rumbles and cracks of lightning and afterwards hear the birds and insects again, making the most of their newly drenched surroundings.

The chill returns by **October**, those huddled particles again framing city acoustics: cries of *Evening Standard* sellers and their idiosyncratic cries of 'Staann-uh' or 'Fiiina' (admittedly less enthusiastic now that they're giving it away); the sales pitch of your regular *Big Issue* seller, wrapped up against the cold. Buses whoosh through puddles, buskers warble in underpasses and sales patters come to the fore – from geezers selling gladioli in Columbia Road to jaunty lads touting reggae CDs, goat jerky and a few other products better off whispered at Brixton Market.

Most distinctive, though, are the sounds of wind sweeping through tunnels in the Underground, the rattles of the trains, the beep of closing doors and station announcers placating passengers and mocking fools who jam the doors. On a rammed Piccadilly Line recently, the enlightened driver began to quote Gandhi: 'There's more to life than increasing its speed.' Beyond his message, it was a moment of nostalgia: apparently, the message was part of Art on the Underground, and in particular a project encouraging drivers to speak out once more, 'provoking thought on life in the city' over the loudspeaker.

Fireworks at the Lord Mayor's Show and Bonfire Night in early **November** make sure autumn ends with a bang not a whimper. There's no better view of the fireworks than from Victoria Embankment, Waterloo or Blackfriars Bridges, their bright dance reverberating along the Thames. Listen to the wind rustling the last leaves off the trees, and try to differentiate between different shapes and ages. On tree-lined streets, notice how the lunchtime rush increases the improvised jazz-drummer swish of leaves underfoot.

If the 'cha-ching' of Christmas consumerism and the omnipresent shopping Muzak drives you to drink in **December**, then clink glasses and sing merrily. Choirs take to streets – we love the Trafalgar Square series, particularly when the choir of St Martin-in-the-Fields step outside their home to fill the lamp-lit, pine-scented sky – and churches citywide let loose with Handel's *Messiah*. Grab a pew at your favourite church, or venture across to St John's in Smith's Square, now a dedicated music venue where the baroque, vaulted grandeur provides a most uplifting and transcendental experience.

And when feeling suitably reflective after your seasonal excess, seek out silence (and the essay later in this chapter).

Staged Sounds

London's natural rhythm is about music as much as birdsong; it shapes our character and guides our tempo. Going to see local bands in Camden or art school students creating noise can be just as 'slow' as listening to a classical recital by the Philharmonic or gathering around a piano for an old-fashioned knees-up. It's about connecting with time and place. There are any number of venues but some, we suggest, are just a little 'slower' than others.

Many of our historic theatres and music halls are endangered. Some, like the Camden Theatre and Brixton Academy, survive (through nightclub crowds and O2 sponsorship respectively), others close, and more struggle on.

Wilton's Music Hall in Graces Alley, east London *(020 7702 2789; www.wiltons.org. uk)* is the world's oldest surviving music hall, built by John Wilton in 1858 behind his pub, The Prince of Denmark. In its time the hall has been a warehouse, bomb shelter and Methodist mission but it has only just survived 80 years of relative dereliction as a small-scale venue staging anything from opera to theatre.

On the opposite side of town is **Bush Hall** *(310 Uxbridge Rd, Shepherds Bush; 020 8222 6955; www.bushhallmusic.co.uk)*, an Edwardian dance hall that hit its stride in the swinging 1930s. Like Wilton's, it has suffered many indignities (Bingo!) over the years but is being revitalised as a music venue that brings together the best of old and new and is part of a continuous musical thread that links traditional variety acts to today's cutting edge.

Churches all over town are doubling as music venues, many providing free lunchtime concerts and rehearsals where you can stroll in for a little everyday transcendence. Every Thursday and Friday night the 350-year old crypt below **St Giles Church** in Camberwell *(020 7701 1016; www.jazzlive.co.uk)* comes alive – relax, we mean metaphorically – with world music and jazz by candlelight respectively. It is thanks to a progressive parish vicar and a mystery donor who bestowed what was first thought to be sticks of dynamite but turned out to be tubes of rather valuable antique coins. **The Union Chapel** *(Compton Tce; 020 7226 1686; www.unionchapel.org. uk)* by Highbury Corner in Islington has gone the whole hog, becoming a full-time music venue. The beautiful interior of the 135-year-old Victorian Gothic church, along with stone pulpit and a stained-glass rose window, provides a stunning backdrop for performers, the staff are unfailingly friendly and proceeds go to charities.

And we just couldn't *not* mention the **Barbican** *(Silk St; 020 7638 4141; www.barbican. org.uk)*, behind the unlikely concrete façade of which you'll find spaces ranging from the 200-seat Pit Theatre to the 1949-seat Barbican Hall and an unfailingly engaging programme from dance and theatre to music, art and film. This site has a special place in London's aural heritage, as it was once home to John Warner and Sons, the foundry where Big Ben was cast in 1856.

Searching for Silence

Interludes of quiet are essential for the slow life. However, as a native Londoner, it is debatable whether I have ever heard true silence. Instead, over the years, I have learnt to find my own quiet and even when squeezed into the busiest of Northern Line carriages, as long as I have a suitably transporting book I can block out the jarring clatter of London and find a modicum of peace.

It is a problem Reverend Nagase well understands. A monk of the Nipponzan Myohoji Buddhist order, he has been in charge of the Battersea Park Peace Pagoda since he helped build it in 1984. I grew up in Battersea and can recall the Thameside encampment of nuns and monks who worked 12 hours a day, seven days a week to construct the Pagoda, which looks as gleaming and incongruous today as it did 25 years ago.

It is a peaceful spot, particularly on a damp Thursday morning when the park is empty but for the hardiest of dog walkers. The noise of the never-ending traffic on the opposite embankment is only a low rumble and the sky is filled with the song of the birds who inhabit the lofty parade of Horse Chestnut trees. The wood and stone structure houses four relief sculptures of the golden Buddha, illustrating his birth, his enlightenment, preaching and finally his passing. It was while contemplating this image, the serene Sidhartha lying on his side with his eyes closed, that I was met by the Reverend. He was walking in the rain in his orange robes, a lit incense stick in his hand and a little cloth bag over his shoulder.

He beat his drum and sang his prayers before inviting me back to his 'hut', in fact a pleasant bungalow set in a shadowy garden. Inside is the Temple, a room heavy with incense and decorated with more golden statues of Buddha, wall hangings, bells and flowers; surely one of the most tranquil places in the capital.

'Today people are too clever and scientific, they are always thinking and questioning. It would be better to be more simple and humble, not to argue so much, but to be gentle and respectful of other humans, that way there will be less fighting and more peace,' explains the Reverend as we kneel on cushions. He recommends prayer as a simple and effective route to inner quiet and spiritual wellbeing. 'To meditate is hard, you need silence and training, but it is easy to put the hands together and pray, you can do it anywhere, even in a crowded, noisy place, and immediately your mind is elevated and finds the Buddha.'

But you don't have to be a Buddhist to find peace at the Pagoda. The Reverend tells me about the many people he encounters cycling to work when he is at his 6am prayer, most of them going out of their way to pass the monument. 'They say it is helpful to them to come this way, to see the Pagoda at the beginning of their day.' Indeed, when I was living in Battersea during my twenties, I loved my evening run along the river and past the Pagoda. It was certainly not quiet – on a golden summer evening this place hums with life,

with the joggers, pram-pushers, romancing couples and businessmen on their mobile phones – but among the throngs the sight of the Pagoda reminds one to empty the mind of all its competing thoughts just for a moment.

Religious locations are generally excellent places to find quiet, and London has thousands of churches. However, a suburban, out-of-the-way one, like the lovely neo-Gothic St Stephen's on College Road in leafy Sydenham, is a better bet than some of London's more famous offerings. St Paul's Cathedral is possibly one of the noisiest places in town. A whisper in its famed 'Whispering Gallery' can be heard 32 metres away on the opposite side of the Dome; and on a busy day there's a lot of whispering.

Someone who was really serious about silence could sign up as a Benedictine monk. The order has a monastery affiliated to Ealing Abbey where, apart from the two daily recreation periods after breakfast and lunch, 'casual conversation' is kept to a minimum. 'Silence is seen not as a prohibition on talking but rather as permitting an openness to God.'

But what can London offer the citizen who wants a more secular silence? A friend who is going through a particularly gruesome divorce told me the quietest place she has ever encountered in London is the garden in Middle Temple's Fountain Court at the Inns of Court. This garden is open to the public at lunchtime during the summer months, but for the rest of the year its cloistered quiet is reserved for the barristers and their clients. 'It had been the most awful day, and my barrister told me to sit in this one spot, in front of the fountain and under the ancient mulberry tree. I have never been anywhere like it, it was so incredibly peaceful, and I was able to stop thinking about all my problems and relax for the first time in an age. I totally lost track of time. It was wonderful.'

London can be a stressful city; fast, noisy and unrelenting, but amongst all its bluster there are restful pockets where the weary urbanite can stop and take stock. Those peaceful places are all the more magical through their contrast with the madness of the city to which they belong. ❧

Gavanndra Hodge

smell

SCENTS AND LOCAL SENSIBILITY

> **YOU'RE ONLY HERE FOR A SHORT VISIT. DON'T HURRY, DON'T WORRY. AND BE SURE TO SMELL THE FLOWERS ALONG THE WAY.**
>
> Walter Hagen

There's no other sense as instinctive, emotive or imaginative as smell. The hint of a familiar scent can cast us back to childhood summers, provide succour in times of stress and be positively intoxicating when we least expect it.

As newborns recognise their mothers by scent, perhaps Londoners too get an innate sense of belonging from the familiar scents of our hometown. 'It's very animal,' says perfumer James Craven of smell. 'It's fully formed and fully operative from the moment we're born, warning us and governing us, but that's less relevant these days so we're perpetually confused by it. It's a mystery, it doesn't have it's own language so we have to use other adjectives to describe it.'

Sure, most Londoners could find countless apt adjectives to describe the sweaty Tube or the open door of a fish and chip shop but flare your nostrils a little and you'll discover a potpourri of more pleasant and natural scents waiting to please and tease. Some can be savoured year-round, while others are fleeting and instinctively tie us to time and place.

The Eau Almanac

On 1 **January** we hold our noses in the air and contemplate the year ahead. The fresh, still air of winter frames an olfactory symphony (even if it sometimes feels more like a violent clanging than an orchestra. 'Like so much else about the city, the smell of London is very closed in,' admits 'perfume archivist' James Craven of Les Senteurs, the UK's oldest independent perfumery *(71 Elizabeth St; www.lessenteurs.co.uk)*.

'There's a certain usedness about the smell,' says James, 'a slight recycledness; there's petrol and bus fumes and cigarettes but mixed with that there are wonderful smells like warm wildflowers, for example in those great beds around Buckingham Palace. Smell is such a vivid, basic instinct, and a mass of contradictions, so it can take you by surprise.'

February passes with a glacial slowness, when 'bookshops come to mind,' says James, 'and the smell of paperbacks and newspaper, so much disposable paper in the city.' But there are also timeless leather-bound classics, with thick ink and musty pages; nothing soothes like a cosy afternoon browsing in a favourite second-hand bookshop (rich oak shelves and dusty rarities), or settling into a log-fire pub to read.

For some February is represented by the smell of a warming evening at the flicks: buttery popcorn, worn velvet seats and the crook of a loved one's neck. Outdoors, the winter rain brings out the remote earthy trace of new mud on the playing fields, and later the damp leather perfume of boots and shoes drying in the corner.

Snowdrops push their way through the ground as the frost clears, their delicate honey scent signalling spring. They're joined by the yellow smell (how else could you describe it?) of freshly cut daffodils that seems to be everywhere, and there are some five million bulbs flowering at the Royal Botanical Gardens alone. But it all pales in comparison to the lead-up to Valentine's Day at Columbia Road Flower Market. Huguenots settled in east London in the 18th and 19th centuries, bringing an expertise in textiles and a love of fresh-cut flowers. Of course, east London boys run the show now; their cockney cries ring out and add to the sensory din, which includes the reek of tall stories ('So fresh you can still see the morning dew on 'em jonquils, love,' touts one chap as he stashes away his spray bottle).

Comfort eating marks **March**. Hot cross buns were almost banned for being too Catholic but reprieved by Elizabeth I for Easter only, thank God. Fishmongers gear up to their Good Friday busiest (and stinkiest). Fresh fish shouldn't smell, but en masse there's no avoiding it, and selling nothing but flapping-fresh seafood, Billingsgate Fish Market has a distinctive pong. The sweet smell of cocoa completes Easter's trifecta.

Come **April** we emerge into the brightening, lengthening light with senses keenly alert. Men rhapsodise about the smell of freshly cut grass at the Oval or football ground: it makes their senses tingle with potential and evokes a sense of triumphalism and even tribalism. In the back garden, it

WORKING THROUGH THE CROWD AT COLUMBIA ROAD

FORAGING FOR FUNGI AT HAMPSTEAD HEATH

evokes a sense of achievement, of a chore completed and a well-earned beer in the sun, itself smelling malty, yeasty and oh-so-sweet.

Brick Lane closes for a day in **May** for the Bengali New Year celebrations, Baishakhi Mela, and the narrow street fills with the hum of black mustard seeds, cardamom, fenugreek, curry leaves, cumin, coriander and lots of sugar. Equally evocative, but in striking contrast, is the RHS Chelsea Flower Show. 'You have to mention the smell of roses,' James insists. Some 400 varieties are in bloom at this time in the Queen Mary's Garden in Regent's Park, emitting a romantic, syrupy haze. Elsewhere, herb and apothecary gardens, like the Old Operating Theatre and Herb Garrett on the South Bank, are in full aromatic bloom; crush the leaves of rosemary, mint and thyme and breathe in the bouquet.

'There is a particular smell in the parks in **June**, the smell of linden blossom mingled with the traffic,' says James. The warm air can amplify unfortunate city smells, but this citrus tang cuts through the air like nothing else. 'In recent years as we've had hotter days, there's the occasional bush of jasmine, mixed up in a haze of petrol. There are some in Caledonian Rd near where I live, some in Jermyn St, this incredibly sweet smell; you could be in Damascus but then there's a great waft of exhaust as a background to it, bringing you right back to London.'

Barbeque and burning sausages waft over garden fences in **July**, coaxing us to leave work early and take sudden interest in our work/life balance. Lidos emit a pleasantly antiseptic air (not requiring as much chlorine as indoor pools) and the smell of your skin after a bracing plunge is invigorating in itself. Resin from the capital's conifers also releases its relaxing fragrance when it warms up – if you find a golden chunk on a tree trunk, save it for adding to a log fire later in the year.

In late summer, says James, after a long dry spell, 'you get the extraordinary smell

A Whiff of the Past

London's memory is filled with fragrances past. As the city expanded between the 17th and 19th centuries, its famous fog was acrid and thickened by countless coal fires; whale blubber burned in street lamps, vegetables rotted around the stocks, and industry brought a whole raft of new odours.

Fleet St was pungent with printers' ink and the hot metal and paper of the presses. Tea, coffee and tobacco were distributed from warehouses and wharfs along the Thames, while Bermondsey smelled of Hartley's jam. Tate and Lyle have been refining sugar in Silvertown, Newham since the 19th century, and residents will tell you it's not as sweet as you'd think.

The capital was the source of most of Britain's gin, with 75 distillers dousing the city in juniper at the start of the 19th century. Meanwhile, the East End was soaked in competing whiffs from Truman's and Whitbread breweries. Nowadays the only major brewer in London is Fullers, sending the yeasty, hoppy blast out to residents of Chiswick.

of the cold rain hitting hot pavements.' **August** rains awaken the flat, musty odour of London stone that seeps from the very walls and roads. (In underpasses and stairwells a somewhat sharper tang might be added to the smell, in which case a sudden acceleration is more than acceptable.) It all collides at Notting Hill Carnival, revelling in the atmosphere of spices, booze and fumes from generators and joints.

Autumn, Keats' bucolic season of mists and mellow fruitfulness, fleets like no other season. In **September** fruit from apple trees drops to pavements all over suburbia and ferments, while markets have the year's richest haul of produce. The earthy odours of wild mushrooms rise up from Hampstead Heath, their woody, fungal scent belying the hot buttered sizzle they'll emit in the kitchen later on (see p116).

For more unusual natural smells in **October**, head to Kew gardens where Algerian Oak releases its sweet fragrance and the dead and decaying foliage of the Katsura tree smells like candyfloss. Trodden, damp drifts of leaves coat the streets, provoking James' description of Leicester Square: 'A ghastly, hot burning sweet sugar smell, like candy floss.' It's an unusual description of autumn streets, but either he's spot on, or we're terribly suggestible. Love it or loathe it, that's the beauty of the sense, says James. 'We *see* the same, our hearing is the same, but our noses are so individually arranged, the sense of smell is very idiosyncratic. It's endlessly interpreted by different people.'

Statistically, **November** is the wettest month and the dousing of rain swells the Thames, cloying us with a part-nice, part-dirty sock collision of fermentation and cleansed air. More pleasant odours await on street corners in the West End: caramel nut roasters snag passers-by with their sweet scent. The smell of soggy homespun fireworks and smouldering bonfires (burning wood laced with a trace of tyre rubber to be precise) distinguish Guy Fawkes Night. Public parks like Battersea, Brockwell and Ravenscourt stage proper festivities, where the smoke from the bonfires mingle with the nostalgic hum of mulled wine, smoky chestnuts and trampled masses of late autumn leaves.

December is a series of sweet-smelling treats. 'I love the smell of stores,' says James, 'that airlessness mixed with leather and perfume. It's distinctive of London.' In the timber-polish confines of Burlington Arcade you'll find two of the city's oldest shoemakers, Churches and Crockett and Jones, both more than 100 years old and opportunities to step back in time. Equally extravagant, Penhaligon's is the place for some old-fashioned English Fern aftershave (as long as you're not repelled by the sniffy atmosphere).

Every year since 1947 a thank-you card arrives from Norway in the shape of a 50-year-old, 25-metre high Norwegian spruce. The 'queen of the forest' takes pride of place on the city's mantelpiece, Trafalgar Square, and its pine needles bring a hint of the snowbound Norwegian forests to central London. Kew arborists, however, prefer local flowering plants such as winter honeysuckles. Lavender, though in bloom year-round, seems ever more fragrant and calming against winter's cool, clear canvas.

Wrapping up the olfactory year are nips of whisky, proper roast dinners and perhaps the metaphorical whiff of bull as New Year's resolutions are enunciated.

The Big Smoke

My dad started smoking at seven, back in the day when cigarettes 'cured' coughs and colds. The smouldering my mother once noticed on a date with him was traced not to his glances, but to the lit pipe stashed in his jacket pocket. By comparison I was a late starter, smoking my first cigarette at 14. I'm not sure why I started; probably because it gave me something to do while doing nothing in particular.

Without the health-conscious piety of cities like San Francisco or Sydney, there's something fitting about smoking in London: the spark of the lighter and the crackle of the first inhalation suit the city's hedonism. Or perhaps we just like being teased with memories of younger days and longer nights.

But I'm relieved to be an ex-smoker today because the city has declared war on the habit and, in the process, brought 400 years of history undone. Like a disease, smoking arrived here through a chain of sailors. Captain John Hawkins, a privateer and slave trader, brought the first tobacco leaves back from the West Indies in the 1560s, where he introduced Sir Francis Drake to the habit. Drake gave Sir Walter Raleigh his first puff and he, in turn, persuaded Elizabeth I to have a drag. By 1603 doctors were complaining that people were using tobacco to treat, among other ailments, toothache, halitosis and cancer, smoking it in small clay pipes.

James I became London's first anti-smoker. He published *A Counterblaste to Tobacco* in 1604, a spirited if scientifically flawed rant against the 'filthie noveltie' of the 'vile custom', which he argued was 'lothsome to the eye, hatefull to the nose, harmefull to the braine, dangerous to the lungs'. And in case anyone was in any doubt about his feelings he slapped a huge tax on tobacco. Perhaps it was the constant tut-tutting that motivated committed smoker Guy Fawkes to try and take him down (not historically documented but plausible nonetheless). At any rate, the King's efforts were to no avail: the habit was already ingrained in the city's consciousness.

In its day the Tobacco Dock at Porter's Walk, Wapping covered five acres, but today it's a listed but rather sad, empty building, occasionally used as a film set and a party venue. Since the summer of 2007, Mayfair's proud cigar clubs have jumped through hoops to allow smoking on their premises (although City gents might have less to spend on Cohibas and Montecristos lately). But elsewhere across the capital, smoking is being kicked to the pavement. Even the shisha smokers of Edgware Rd have been shunted outside, and few now bother sitting at chilly cafe tables beside the busy road.

I'm in two minds about the ban. On one hand, now we can return from a night at the pub without smelling like we've spent a night in the pub – clearly a good thing. On the other, as Tom Hodgkinson notes, the anti-pleasure policy doesn't chime with our slow sensibility. ❧

taste

CHARACTERISTIC FLAVOURS

> ❝ **GIVE ME SPOTS ON THE APPLES**
> **BUT LEAVE ME THE BIRDS AND THE BEES.** ❞
> Joni Mitchell

Life would be unbearably bland without taste, perhaps the most important sense by which we enjoy the world (and get a grasp of 'slow'). It feels like we've come full circle and are re-appreciating food and drink for its taste and provenance rather than its convenience. Farmers' markets are sprouting up all over and restaurateurs are proudly proclaiming where their produce is sourced. And in such a hectic city, home cooking and family meals are nourishment for the soul.

Eating is one of the few experiences we can share communally and which involves all the senses, so we really should make the most of London's bounty (and not take the whole enterprise so darn seriously).

Slow Food London

The seeds of the slow food movement were sown in 1986 when a McDonald's was slated to open beside the Spanish Steps in Rome. Italian food writer Carlo Petrini decided the culture of fast food had encroached too far and so, brandishing bowls of penne, he led a protest against mass production and the homogenisation of taste.

Petrini and his friends lit spot fires of creative dissent around the world, prompting people to reengage with food and weigh up the real costs of convenience. The official Slow Food organisation has been active in London for more than a decade. Far from being puritanical, people who subscribe to the slow food values are dedicated to pleasure – individual, collective, sustainable, natural, traditional and sensory pleasure.

'Underpinning the slow food philosophy is its long-standing campaign for good, clean and fair food,' explains Catherine Gazzoli, CEO of Slow Food UK. 'Good, because food should taste good. Clean, because food should be produced in a way which fully respects the environment, human health and animal welfare. Fair, because the workers at all stages of production are paid a fair and honest wage.'

It's simple really. Take an apple. Bought at a market in September, when it's been grown locally, naturally and in season, it's a slow food. Plucked from a supermarket shelf out of season, when it's been ripened with chemicals and shipped half way around the world, it's a fast food. Londoners are increasingly interested in where food comes from and how it is produced; buying local, free-range, line-caught, organic food and taking a stance against the dominance of supermarkets is as much of a political statement as voting.

Farmers markets and independent food stores are on the increase, but too often the slow food movement is branded with a reputation of being elitist. 'There is great availability, but prices can be a little higher,' Catherine says, 'but the costs justify a fair wage for workers at all stages of production. The interest is there for the slow food philosophy of good, clean and fair food, and we need to make this accessible for everyone.'

In recent years London has been at the forefront of a back-to-basics form of cookery, such as the concept of nose-to-tail eating. A pair of great London chefs, Marco Pierre White and Fergus Henderson, made it acceptable, fashionable even, for top-class restaurants to serve pigs' trotters or offal. And with finances tight, cheaper cuts are more popular still (and definitely slower to cook).

Eating is filled with ethical dilemmas when you think about it. How much fossil fuel was required to transport that banana? What cruelty was inflicted to produce that chop or those eggs? How many poor people were exploited to harvest the cocoa beans for your chocolate bar? How many chemicals does it take to produce a perfectly shiny red pepper? And did I just eat the last Orange roughy? It's a lot to think about – almost enough to put you off your food if there wasn't a simple way to be part of the cure; simply by being more mindful about where your food and drink comes from.

Filling your Basket

We all enjoy the convenience of a supermarket but buying from a market, deli or greengrocer and supporting a local business feels infinitely more rewarding. Shopping's more fun when it includes a wink and grin from the purveyor, who'll probably know you by name and proudly recommend the day's best cut or the crunchiest radishes he's had all season. So if a locally owned shop or stallholder has the same item for a few pennies more than the big chains, try thinking of it as a form of community upkeep.

Better still is to buy organic. Sure, it costs more to wait for nature to take its course rather than to artificially hurry the process, but when you factor in the benefits to health, community, environment and flavour, it starts to seem like a bargain. Besides, organics are not actually that much more expensive if you shop at markets and buy what's in season.

MARKETS Unlike the often irradiated, bland and shrink-wrapped veggies piled high on supermarket shelves, the produce at farmers markets is bursting with flavour and freshness. Many markets have become buzzing community gatherings where we get to slow down without even thinking about it – meet the people who produce our food, chat about what's in season, get tips on how to cook and combine different produce, and discover new and old flavours that we lost in the bright lights of the supermarket aisle.

There are 15 weekly markets managed by **London Farmers Markets** *(020 7833 0338; www.lfm.org.uk)*, from Acton to Wimbledon. The producers at these markets come from within 100 miles of the M25 and make, grow, raise or shoot everything they sell – there are strictly no middlemen. These strict rules mean you won't find bananas or olives, but you will get sweet and crunchy carrots with soil still attached or apples with slight blemishes designed by nature and rejected by central buyers, honey straight from the hive, meats, cheeses and freshly baked bread. If

you don't have a local farmers market, the **Marylebone Farmers Market** *(Cramer St carpark)* is worth crossing town for. Even Slow Food London recommends it and they don't give out recommendations lightly (however hard we cajole them).

Farmers markets have the best slow credentials, but any option that shortens the supply chain and gives the consumer more control is good in our book. If it's been grown, reared, filleted, cured or baked by someone proud of their craft – people like Flour Power City, whose hand-made bread is fully organic – all the better. **Borough Market** *(Stoney St; www.boroughmarket.org.uk)* has been held on the same site on Thursdays, Fridays and Saturdays for the past 250 years. Underneath the wrought ironwork, stallholders lay out hand-dived scallops, wild mushrooms and whole cured hams. Most are only too pleased to give you a taste of their aged stilton, thyme-marinated olives or fresh-pressed Bramley apple juice ('You can taste the tang from that cold snap we had in July!').

Slow Food London hosts an infrequent **Slow Food Market** *(www.slowfoodlondon.*

blogs.com) in the courtyard of the Southbank Centre, which brings some of the best artisan producers into contact with local foodies, and encourages discussion about the way we eat in London. 'The market itself provides a forum not only for selling cooked and raw produce,' explains Catherine Gazzoli, 'but for cookery demonstrations, discussions on food and a forum for other like-thinking organisations like Pestival, River of Flowers, Sustain and the Soil Association to reach out and talk to the public.'

BAKERS Nothing compares to fresh-baked bread for on-the-spot contentment, and who can resist the rich, comforting smell of crusty loaves emanating from the oven? Which makes it all the more ludicrous that we put up with so much bland, plastic-wrapped rubbish in recent years.

'There are more and more decent bakeries popping up in London these days,' says Eamonn Sweeney, and it takes one to know one. In south London, Eamonn has three brilliant little **Blackbird Bakeries** *(Herne Hill at 208 Railton Rd; Crystal Palace at 71 Westow St; and East Dulwich at 46 Grove Vale)*, all stocked with handmade bread from his 4 and 20 Bakery on Milkwood Rd. He was inspired to start Blackbird after working at the renowned Blackdog Bakery in Martha's Vineyard. 'America was well ahead but I started with a market stall, which was amazingly successful and proved there was an appetite for artisan bread here. In 2003 I opened the first shop.' Blackbird's shelves are stacked with sourdough, rye and flavoured breads, with 200 loaves baked nightly: 'All are made from scratch by hand, that's the most important thing,' he says.

Baking bread might mean an all-night shift – Eamonn starts baking at 11pm and doesn't finish until 5 or 6am – but, hours aside, it's a uniquely slow enterprise. You can't rush the process. 'I have a big bucket of sourdough starter and as long as I keep feeding it with flour and water every day it will keep going.'

The **Old Post Office Bakery** *(76 Landor Rd, Clapham; www.oldpostofficebakery.co.uk)* started baking organic bread long before it was popular. It all started in a Brixton squat before gradually moving up the chain to this trendy new postcode, but the tiny bakery is still as unfussy and delicious as ever. They use Gloucestershire flour to experiment with a range of sourdoughs, traditional whole-wheats, specialty breads and cakes but nothing beats their chocolate fudge brownies – organic means guilt-free, right?

For more glamorous bread-breaking occasions, pick up a loaf from the counter at St John Bread and **Wine in Spitalfields** *(94–96 Commercial St; www.stjohnbreadandwine.com)*, a 2003 spin-off from Fergus Henderson's St John restaurant (p118). Or better still, stay for a breakfast of a Gloucester Old Spot bacon sandwich or eggy bread with syrup.

Of course, man cannot live by bread alone; a coffee and cupcake also go down well. The delightful little **Hummingbird Bakery** in Notting Hill *(133 Portobello Rd; 020 7229 6446; www.hummingbirdbakery.com)* started in 2004 as a reaction against bland cakes and calorie-counting wowsers, armed with simple old-fashioned recipes, buttercream icing and tonnes of sprinkles. We'll do our bit for the cause. Seasonal cupcakes are a real treat; our favourite is a summer blueberry and cream that will warp glycaemic levels for the rest of the day.

BUTCHERS Finding and befriending a good local butcher, who knows the source of every item on display, is key to eating well in London. Although a little, ahem, rare these days the best of them attract shoppers from all over the capital.

Many source their cuts from the **Smithfield Meat Market** (*Charterhouse St*), and while it's not the most welcoming place for a weekly shop, visit at least once to get a sense of how seriously the city takes the trade. The beautiful Victorian building has been standing since 1866 – a welcome architectural distraction for the weaker-stomached when wandering past filleting stations and whole carcasses – although livestock has been traded here since the 10th century.

The Guild of Q Butchers (*www.guildofqbutchers.com*) lists some of the city's finest meatmen. Naturally, most are organic: free of antibiotics and growth hormones, coming from well-kept animals that eat pesticide-free feed. Organic may cost a little more but, as Allegra McEvedy, London's most effervescent chef points out, a good butcher will recommend cheaper cuts and how to cook them. At any rate, what you lose in your pocket you make up for in taste, wholesomeness and peace of mind. Although the industry would hardly thank us for suggesting it, perhaps we should be aiming to eat better meat, less often.

Sheepdrove Organic Farm is a family-run farm based on the Berkshire Downs, selling its organic produce from its shop in Maida Vale (*5 Clifton Rd; 020 7266 3838; www.sheepdrove.com*) on a street that has several independent foodstores. The Kindersleys lead the way in pesticide and chemical-free farming to Soil Association standards. They're also happy to recommend cheaper cuts such as shin or shoulder and offer seasonal meat, such as mutton in autumn.

A Clapham favourite, **M Moen and Sons** (*24 The Pavement; 020 7622 1624; www.moen.co.uk*) has a hog roast at weekends (be warned of the Saturday crowds, although service is efficient) but fabulous free-range chickens, seasonal game, beef, lamb and pork are the best reasons to visit. They can tell you everything from what the chickens are fed to how long the beef has been hung for (and don't expect the short story). They're also a good source of things you won't find in supermarkets such as offal or game birds.

Marylebone's Ginger Pig (*8–10 Moxon St; 020 7935 7788; www.thegingerpig.co.uk*) is named after the rust-coloured Tamworth pig, an old English breed. Founder Tim Wilson raises them on three farms in Yorkshire and even grows his own feed rather than use artificial foods. Originally, the Ginger Pig sold only sausages at Borough Market, but the enterprise has expanded to include this shop in Marylebone, a new shop in Hackney (*99 Lauriston Rd; 020 8986 6911*), another in Waterloo (*inside the Greensmiths supermarket*) and a full range of traditionally-reared meats, including Texel and Dorset lamb and Longhorn beef.

The original **Frank Godfrey** (*7 Highbury Park; 020 7226 9904; www.fgodfrey.co.uk*) would be pleased to know that, four generations on, his shop is still in the family. Now a cornerstone of the community, the shop still proudly sells the same high quality of additive-free meat as Frank did 100 years ago, back when he grazed his cattle by license on Clissold Park.

taste...

FISHMONGERS

There's nothing slow about the decline in the world's fish stocks, and shopping for sustainably sourced fish today is easier said than done. Wild or farmed? Line-caught or trawled? Getting the facts to make an informed choice is harder than ever. **The Marine Conservation Society** *(www.mcsuk.org)* produces a free Good Fish Guide listing the status of the most popular species; the information is also available at www.fishonline.org. At last count there were 69 species on their fish to avoid list, from anchovy to turbot. **The Marine Stewardship Council** *(www.msc.org)* is a London-based charity that certifies fish and fish products – look for its logo on packaging.

In Islington **Steve Hatt** *(88–90 Essex Rd; 020 7226 3963)* has a peerless reputation for his fish and can claim to be London's best fishmonger – although he's far too modest to do such a thing. Saturdays are busiest, when people travel from all over to see what's come in on the boats. As Steve points out, the way to tell a good fishmonger is whether you can smell it down the street; flapping-fresh fish doesn't smell. The shop has been in the family since 1895 when it began life as a smokehouse; Steve still sells shop-smoked haddock, trout and mackerel.

Independent fishmongers can afford to be pickier about where their stock comes from and are also able to react more quickly to seasonal changes. The charming **Moxon's** in Clapham *(Westbury Parade, Nightingale Lane; 020 8675 2468)* sells the freshest of fish, expertly filleted on request. Keep an eye out for the mussels and other seafood specials. Towards the east, the **Sea Cow** in Dulwich *(37 Lordship Lane; 020 8693 3111;* *www.theseacow.co.uk)* is a posh fish and chip shop, but we go for the wet fish counter selling sustainably sourced fish such as line-caught cod and yellowfin tuna.

GROCERS AND DELIS

Just the word 'greengrocer' evokes notions of frill-free and long established places where staff are keen to please and greet regulars by name. Most are struggling to compete against supermarkets, as you can imagine, but a few are holding their ground and being propped up by appreciative local communities. Like conscientious Finchley stalwart Gary Ellingham, proprietor of **TJ Ellingham and Sons** *(Ballards Lane)*. Gary was born into the 60-year-old business, inherited from his father and is still doing everything the old-fashioned, conscientious way of previous generations.

Even older is **W Martyn** *(135 Muswell Hill Broadway; 020 8883 5642)*, a family-owned teashop and grocer that retains the character of 1897. You'll find jars of pickles, condiments and treats piled high on old timber shelves, while pounds of sugar and nuts are weighed on old balance scales. This was an everyday grocer a century ago – a proud one, mind – but times have changed so much that we now call these fine foods and punters are lured in with the smell of coffee being roasted.

Other mindful retailers are capitalising on the demand for organic, artisan fare. **Farm W5** *(19 The Green, High St, Ealing; 020 8566 1965; www.farmw5.com)* calls itself a grocer, but it's more like a great slow supermarket, a place for some 50 small growers and producers to sell their wares. 'Throughout the week Richard brings us his meat from his farm in Devon. Once a week Ian and Sue send someone in with our amazing handmade pies. Paul buys our veg, Tony has the bread to bake, Will milks his cows. Once a month Tom pops to see Ginny for our muesli, oats and flour. Terry comes with the jam as often as she can. And someone is nearly always coming in with a cheese.'

The Natural Kitchen in Marylebone *(77–78 Marylebone High St; 020 7486 8065; www.thenaturalkitchen.com)* is another new venture offering artisan, organic and wild produce. There's a good-looking meat counter and upstairs is a friendly cafe, which warms the cockles with seasonal, free-range and flavoursome fare.

The aroma of farmhouse cheeses from around the British Isles is immediately appetising at **Neal's Yard Dairy** *(17 Shorts Gardens, Covent Garden and 6 Park St, Borough; 020 7240 5700; www.nealsyarddairy. co.uk)*. Many are matured in-house until they reach their peak, at which point queues of cheese lovers line up like groupies at a gig. It can take a wheel of Stilton more than six months to mature but that's a blink of the eye to fellow cheese specialists **Paxton & Whitfield** *(93 Jermyn St; 020 7930 0259; www. paxtonandwhitfield.co.uk)*, who have been based in St James for more than 200 years. While half the fun of food shopping is prodding, squeezing and sniffing, signing up to a box-delivery service such as **Abel and Cole** *(www.abelandcole.co.uk)* replaces that with an element of surprise and a joyful surrender to nature's whim.

Whether this system will reduce your food miles depends on where and how you shop already. It's a bit like the old-time charm and convenience of having a pint of milk delivered to your doorstep – and for that, there are still plenty of milkmen around town too; www.delivermilk.co.uk will help put you in touch with one.

Minding your Beeswax

While their country cousins are having a hard time, apparently London's honeybees are in clover. And lavender. And buddleia. 'London is really quite green, with parks and small gardens dotted around,' says Orlando Clarke, who has been keeping bees in Brixton for more than 10 years. 'There's usually something in bloom all year round and less insecticide and pesticide being used.' Orlando's **Pure London Honey** *(www.purelondonhoney.com)* is sold at Petersham Garden Nurseries (p119) and the Blackbird Bakery in Herne Hill (p110).

At The **Hive Honey Shop** *(93 Northcote Rd; 020 7924 6233; www.thehivehoneyshop.co.uk)* in Clapham you can see inside a five-foot high, glass-fronted working beehive and get expert and entertaining tuition from head beekeeper, James. The honey itself is royal standard and the preferred spread of the Queen so you might want to take some home (presuming that you're not the Queen, in which case someone will have already stocked the larder, ma'am). Bee expert **Alison Benjamin** *(www.urbanbees.co.uk)*, author of *Keeping Bees and Making Honey*, keeps several hives around London and offers beekeeping courses to wannabe apiarists.

CHILLING AT BOROUGH MARKET

Wild Bounty

Fergus Drennan, aka the **Road Kill Chef** *(www.wildmanwildfood.co.uk)*, survives on a largely foraged diet. 'I'm out there foraging because I want to pick and touch and feel and taste,' he says. 'It seems so obvious and normal to live like this, to counter the high-speed world with go-slow foraging.' Although Fergus lives in Kent, where it's easier to forage, the reasons are just just as valid inside the M25 and there are plenty of opportunities.

Don't be shy about picking overhanging apples, pears and plums from trees beside suburban streets. Gorse (great for wine, cordial and even cakes) and blackberries can be picked on **Blackheath**; there's chervil and garlic on **Walthamstow** marshes; while **Hampstead Heath** is nature's larder with fruit, plants and wild mushrooms galore. Autumn is the main harvest time but you can also enjoy elderflower in June and chestnuts in November, when parks and gardens everywhere are brimming.

A Foraging Foray

'There are about 50 nasties,' advises our guide, 'and it's best to get to know their families and avoid them entirely.' Although it sounds like a tour of gangland London, we're actually on a mushroom-hunting expedition at Hampstead Heath one Sunday morning in Autumn with Andy Overall *(www.fungitobewith.org)*.

There are about 25 in our group – some people have brought their kids, other clutch their wicker baskets expectantly, I try not to be distracted by the keep-fit class doing star jumps on the dewy grass next to us. In truth, I don't have high expectations. Mushrooms like chanterelles and nutty ceps are found in rural woodland, not central London, right?

'We've got about 3000 species of fungi in the UK, and about 200 are of varying degrees of edibility,' says Andy. 'We typically find 100 to 150 varieties up on Hampstead Heath alone. The easiest family to get to know is the boletus (or ceps). We're not the only ones trying to get them though: slugs, squirrels, deer and the Europeans are great at foraging so you're up against it. I couldn't work out why Richmond Park had no ceps until I realised that the place is heaving with deer.'

After handing round some unmistakeably inedible fungi – with unforgettable names like 'destroying angel' – Andy explains that although there's no general rule on identifying poisonous mushrooms, the truly bad ones can be spotted quite easily. He encourages us to use all our senses: sniff the mushroom, prod it, even lick it. A bit of detective work might help us recognise varieties too: 'It's good to know your native trees – oak, birch, willow, beech – as they develop symbiotic relationships with certain species,' says Andy.

And with that we meander off, zigzagging this way and that, our heads bent towards the ground much like bloodhounds in search of a scent. I spot another seasoned mushroom hunter, Carolyn Naish, who lives on the corner of the Heath, and tag along in the hope she'll share some favourite grounds. 'If you'd said to me a few years ago that I would be going for four-hour walks on the Heath I'd have said you were mad,' she tells me. 'Then I went on a foray and was hooked. I love it. You're really excited afterwards and on a high.'

Some of our fellow foragers are ticking off species as if on safari, but Carolyn and I have less noble motivations: our appetite. 'Some people are into the Latin but I do it for my stomach. Keep it simple,' she advises. 'You can't beat a little salt, garlic, butter and cream, if you're feeling flash. In 2006 it was fabulous – I could walk out of my house and fall over mushrooms. Quite often I'll whizz out at midday and have a look for some for lunch. But they all have a value, don't they? They're pretty even if they're not edible.'

One of the more addictive aspects of fungi foraging is that every year is different. 'This year the horn of plenty was out in September, which is very early. The winter chanterelles are just coming out now.' She holds up birch bolete: 'They've not had a great year. They like a hot summer.' Mushrooms, like some people, are triggered by temperature and light. They need an alarm call – wake up mate, or your season is lost!

Where there's a tasty dinner at stake, it seems there's rivalry. 'It's highly competitive,' agrees Carolyn, 'and many of the pickers you see in the woods are very furtive.' Lucky we're more interested in wandering through the Heath and looking at the autumnal light flickering through the trees.

Of course, it's easy to romanticise fungi foraging. Wise foragers know that there's a difference between being *able* to eat something and something actually being worth eating. But there's also an undeniable thrill from eating something you've unearthed yourself, which has been smothered in leaves rather than supermarket packaging.

Back under the canopy of turning leaves, the Heath is giving up its secrets. 'It's so exciting finding a patch of mushrooms and rushing up to Andy – it's like being back at school,' says one forager, Rowan. Everyone, except me has a multi-coloured haul in their rapidly filling baskets. Andy, a fungal oracle, performs the identification rites. There's a coconut-scented milkcap. It's relative, the ugly milkcap, burns like chilli. Someone brings forward a rare find: a mycena pura that smells like radish or incense. There are some examples of the thousands of types of cortinarius, and plenty of clouded agaric mushrooms, temptingly meaty but not edible. Rule one of foraging is to collect the whole of the mushroom because it makes identification much easier.

As a slow day out, fungi foraging has everything: science and foreign languages for the brain, exercise, socialising, natural wonders, seasonality. Everything except, in my case, a mushroom. Then, in a quiet dell, undisturbed by passers by, I find one. It's unmissable. It's unmistakeable. It's a fly agaric. Shiny, red and deadly, it's the poisonous toadstool used, somewhat macabrely, as an illustration in children's books. 'Don't be disheartened,' counsels Carolyn. 'If nothing else, we've all learned something.' That's an understatement: this has been a revelation; there'll be one more regular mushroom hunter next year. ❦

Robin Barton

Not wishing to take the 'fun' out of fungi but do not eat unidentified mushrooms. As Fergus the Forager puts it, all plants and fungi are edible – but some only once.

Eating Out

Recommending places to eat in London is a book in itself, many in fact, each with its own take on what's worth recommending. What's manna to one diner might be a mess to another. What we do know is that the best experiences are when everything comes together: the company, the food, the wine and when you're having so much fun you don't even double-check the bill. Here's a frivolously selective list combining slow criteria like natural, local, traditional, sensory, characteristic and gratifying – places that delight palate, pocket and principle.

RESTAURANTS

The term 'seasonality' is about more than reducing the food miles clocked up by strawberries in winter or oranges in summer; it harks back to simpler times when cooks made the most of what was available (no mean feat in mid-winter). The godfather of mindful Modern British cooking is Fergus Henderson of **St John** *(26 St John St; 020 7251 0848; www.stjohnrestaurant.co.uk)*, who has been championing free-range British produce at his Clerkenwell restaurant for years. Nature writes the menu, he says, if you follow the seasons. St John's plain, whitewashed interior frames Henderson's nose-to-tail reworking of British dishes where no part of the animal is wasted; marrowbones are roasted and calf's liver is served with lentils. Without loudly proclaiming its green credentials, this is real low-impact eating.

With many of the ingredients for **Magdalen's** *(152 Tooley St; 020 7403 1342; www.magdalenrestaurant.co.uk)* menu coming from Borough Market, chefs David Abbott and James and Emma Faulks need only walk five minutes to do the shopping. There's an emphasis on hearty British fare, with seasonal game and unfussy desserts. Meat is sourced from farmer-producers: beef and pork from Hereford and Yorkshire, lamb from North Wales and game from Yorkshire. This cuts down on food miles and supports small, regional caretakers of the land.

Eco-advocate Potts Dawson is chef at the **Acorn House** *(69 Swinton St; 020 7812 1842; www.acornhouserestaurant.com)* and **Water House** *(10 Orsman Rd; 020 7033 0123; www.waterhouserestaurant.co.uk)*, a pair of charitable enterprises owned by the Shoreditch Trust. They're the greenest restaurants in the capital with worm farms, hydro-electric power, deliveries by boat and strict welfare policies for suppliers, which ensure that they leave only the daintiest carbon footprint. Eco-friendly food with a side of charity – man, how much good karma can one place hoard? Uncle Mick Jagger should be proud. And as feared food critic Fay Maschler said, the 'food is jolly good'.

Chef Oliver Rowe of **Konstam at the Prince Albert** *(2 Acton St; 020 7833 5040; www.konstam.co.uk)* has gone further than most in reducing the food miles his trendy Kings Cross restaurant racks up, sourcing his ingredients from within the M25 wherever possible. He found chicken in Waltham Abbey, blue cheese in Norbury and pork in Amersham; in fact, you can take the Tube to most of Rowe's suppliers, proving the locavores right – local can be darn tasty.

CAFES Every culture adds something to London and, arguably, antipodeans have brought great coffee in laidback venues: places like Soho's **Flat White** *(17 Berwick St)* and east London's **Nude Espresso** *(26 Hanbury St)* have become local institutions.

But **Monmouth Coffee Company** *(27 Monmouth St, also at Borough Market; 020 7379 3516; www.monmouthcoffee.co.uk)* stands out. Single-estate beans, from a rotating selection of about a dozen varieties from Africa, Asia, South and Central America, are roasted in Bermondsey, then weighed and ground in the Covent Garden shop. You'll be surprised at the conversation a cuppa invites, when savoured at shared timber tables or perched outside the front window. The shop also sells Sally Clarke's cakes and pastries from iconic foodstore **Villandry** *(www.villandry.com)*.

At **Petersham Garden Nurseries Cafe** *(Petersham Rd, Richmond; 020 8605 3627; www.petershamnurseries.com)*, chef Skye Gyngell picks her largely organic ingredients fresh each day, which is obvious in every lip-smacking bite. And when she can't find what she wants in the herb and vegetable gardens, she sources ingredients from small producers from across the British Isles.

'Expect a relaxed service,' suggests the menu at **Macondo** *(8–9 Hoxton Square)*, a Latin-inspired cafe, bar and gallery that's somehow escaped the usual Shoreditch airs. Works by emerging artists give you something to contemplate over your coffee, while soft beats persuade you into cosy armchairs. Cakes are baked daily with mindful, seasonal ingredients, and for something a little more substantial the slow-cooked stews are wholesome and heartfelt.

Classic Cafes *(www.classiccafes.co.uk)* is more than a review page; it's an homage to the old-school formica cafes that fly in the face of coffee-chain homogeneity. It's all about the 'psychogeography' of the places: 'the hidden landscape of atmospheres, histories, actions and characters which charge environments.' One of our favourites is the Bethnal Green institution, **E. Pellicci** *(332 Bethnal Green Rd)*, which has been serving up the same hearty no-frills grub since 1900. It was a sad day when owner Nevio Pellicci passed away in December 2008; with his neat pencil moustache and crisp shirt and tie, he seemed just as well preserved as the art-deco formica counters. Thankfully Nevio Pellicci Junior is maintaining the tradition of unhurried service and free-flowing chat.

La Vida Locavore

Many of London's slowest restaurants doff their caps to the principles of the international locavore movement, made up of people who eat only what's grown within a 100-mile radius of where they live. Of course, it's just about impossible to maintain and we can get too obsessed with 'food miles' but it's a useful exercise to try for a day. If nothing else, you'll become more conscious of buying local produce and eating seasonally and you'll certainly give greater thanks for the luxuries we ship in.

taste...

There's nothing glamorous about the cafeteria-style tearooms dotted in the middle of parks, which is partly why we love them. Only accessed by a morning meander, they often occupy run-down heritage buildings or have picnic tables from where you can watch the kids and dogs play. Nothing slows like the combination of nature, family and comfort food. We're fickle with our favourites, but particularly partial to the **National Trust** tearooms in Morden Hall Park *(Morden Hall Rd)*, which serve hearty banter with humble, home-baked goodness, mostly sourced from the walled kitchen garden.

The Ritz and the Wolseley are still old London's cup of tea, but a fantastic new addition is **Orange Pekoe** beside the river in Barnes *(3 White Hart Lane; 020 8876 6070; www.orangepekoeteas.com)*, a cosy neighbourhood tearoom selling loose teas including a very refreshing house blend of Darjeeling. Tea here is an art form; each cup is brewed from the heart to provide salve for the soul.

SLOW FAST FOOD No, we haven't lost the plot. Slow food is not about long-simmering casseroles, and take-away parcels – enjoyed in one's own time and place – can often be more slow and gratifying than scheduling a booking. Some chains are better than others (stand up Leon and Gourmet Burger Kitchen) but supporting a local fish and chip shop or pizzeria is rewarding for everybody.

The perfect chip, says expert chipper Harry Niazi of **Olley's** *(65–67 Norwood Rd; 020 8671 8259; www.olleys.info)*, is blanched before being deep-fried so it's crispy on the outside and fluffy on the inside. John Rolfe's secret ingredient in London's best organic sourdough pizza, from **Franco Manca** in Brixton *(4 Market Row, Electric Ave; 020 7738 3021)*, is a little bit of mashed potato in the dough. Now, we're not revealing trade secrets so you can replicate them at home; rather to illustrate that fast food doesn't necessarily equate to thoughtless tucker. Riding a resurgence in the fish and chip industry, perhaps brought on by the need to tighten metaphorical belts, the better chippies these days focus on ethically sourced fish.

'Everybody agrees that there's more awareness than before that you are what you eat,' laughs Allegra McEvedy, 'so if you eat a lot of pies you won't live as long and your sex life won't be as good!' We agree reluctantly; with a side order of mash and liquor, the pie has long been a London staple and giving it up would mean abandoning the traditional tiled pie shops, mostly in south and east London, where customers are called 'love' and regulars earn their own favourite tables. **M Manze** at 105 Peckham High St *(020 7277 6181; www.manze.co.uk)* opened in 1927 and is still baking pies daily. **Harringtons** on Selkirk Rd in Tooting, **Clark's** on Exmouth Market in Clerkenwell and **AJ Goddard** on Deptford High St also deliver cheap and cheerful grub in what can be gorgeous period surroundings: tiled walls, benches, steel worktops and discreet design touches.

Jellied eels are often on pie shops' menus too, although sadly they're far from an ethical choice today, bringing two core slow principles to heads: traditional vs sustainable. Try oysters instead – really! As Sam remarks in Dickens' *The Pickwick Papers* while walking through Whitechapel, there were oyster stalls every half-dozen houses: 'poverty and oysters always seem to go together'.

The Dante Club

'Nel mezzo del cammin di nostra
vita mi ritrovai per una selva oscura
che la diritta via era smarrita.'

'When I had journeyed
half of our life's way,
I found myself within
a shadowed forest,
for I had lost the path
that does not stray.'

It was not quite the middle of my life, but my course had become rather obscured. Nine years ago; three friends and I, all in our mid-twenties, found ourselves jaded with the seemingly infinite round of drinks, parties and dinners that was our social life in London. We decided to do something more fulfilling with our evenings, something with a bit more longevity.

We were all Italianophiles; two of us had studied classics at university, a third Italian, and another had spent a magical year in Florence. And so it was decided that we would get together, once a week, at one of London's many Mediterranean restaurants to read Dante's *Divine Comedy* – all of it, from beginning to end. We knew it would take us years and that was part of the appeal.

Our lives were travelling at such speed that it felt nice to have something that put the brakes on, something that required time and application. Also, as four single girls, it was exciting to think that by the time we got to *Paradiso* our lives would be so different.

The format of the evening was simple, some wine and gossip, followed by a *canto* (about 140 lines). Each of us would read a section in Italian, which we would then translate into English.

I had acquired a lovely Italian edition of *La Divina Commedia* with an illustration of the great man on the cover, staring cleverly into the distance, a white strap under his chin to secure his funny conical hat. Victoria and Verity had bought the edition with the complementary translations, and I soon realised the wisdom of this as I wrestled with esoteric Italian footnotes. But, after three or four bottles of *rosso* my linguistic failings were of no matter; I made my own poetry. As time progressed, so too did my medieval Italian.

The literature was only half the fun; we ate some wonderful food too. Who knew there were was so much fine Italian fare to be had in London? I remember a truffle-infused honey served with parmesan at Aperitivo, a platter of the finest Parma ham at Isola, seabass at Sardo, grilled king prawns and Prosecco at La Famiglia (located in the aptly titled World's End) and creamy wild rabbit gnocchi at Ziani. One of our earliest meetings was at Gordon's wine bar near Embankment, not strictly Italian but the perfect cavernous spot to read about entering the underworld; *'Lasciate ogni speranze, voi ch'intrate'* (All hope abandon, ye who enter in).

Fellow diners may have been perplexed by the lyrical goings-on at our table, but the native waiters loved it. Dante is taught in every school in Italy, and often they would ask to look at the text and sigh and even swoon at the beauty of the lines.

We could not always meet every week, and sometimes a whole month would go by without a session. But it seemed fitting to take the poem at such a slow pace; Dante's own passage through hell, purgatory and paradise was neither quick nor easy, the lesson being that true understanding takes some time.

And I do believe our leisurely approach to the text helped sink it deeper into our brains. Years passed, during which we have had four Dante weddings and three Dante babies (none called Beatrice – yet) and numerous crises and catastrophes. But there was always the poetry, the wine, and the friendship to help us through.

After two years my (now) husband and I took a sabbatical and went to live in the French Pyrennees. The Dante Girls kept going, informing me when they would be meeting and what *canto* we had reached so that I could keep up. In fact, we read the final lines of *Inferno* next to a blazing fire in our mountain retreat; and saw Beelzebub himself with his three heads, featherless wings and tears of bloody foam.

My husband and I came back to London and I renewed my membership of the Dante Club. Six years after we had begun we read the final lines of *Paradiso*. It was a sad day, but we knew it would never be the end. The early Renaissance was a rich time for expansive literature; we dipped our toes into Petrarch's poetry, and now we have started reading Boccaccio's *Decameron*, which will surely last us at least another twenty years. We're not going to rush it. 🐎

Gavanndra Hodge

Drinking

Ever since Geoffrey Chaucer started his pilgrimage to Canterbury from the Tabard Inn in Southwark, pubs have been indispensable to London life – a place to end a day's honest (or dishonest) labour, or even start the day (if you work at Smithfield Market). Everybody has a favourite pub, often dictated by expedience, and there are few better ways to connect with the neighbourhood than over a long, slow pint.

'London has an epic beer history,' says Alastair Hook, arguably the most creative and outspoken brewer in Britain. He'd like to see the city reclaim its mantle as brewing capital of the world. In 1999 he founded the **Meantime microbrewery** in Greenwich *(www.meantimebrewing.com)*, and set out on a mission to banish tasteless fizzy lagers and warm flat ales. Now, he's selling two million pints a year across 13 countries.

The art of a great pint, it turns out, is patience. Where industrial brewers take four or five days, Alastair's beers are brewed over four or five weeks: 'Beer has become quite a hasty affair – the bean counters have got hold of it. If you rush brewing you end up with a less harmonious product with very little hoppy, malty character. We're not part of that world; we're about taste and flavour.'

Hook finds inspiration for his brews throughout the city. To create Meantime's first porter the recipe was researched at the British Library, even using Dickens as a source. Eventually a recipe from 1750 was adapted to incorporate seven malts and Kentish hops. The result is darkly delicious, a chocolate-imbued beer that goes perfectly with oysters.

'We complain about so many things being lost from our culture,' says Alastair, 'yet beer has always been there and we've neglected it.' Alastair is resurrecting an old brewery at the Royal Naval College, which first made beer in 1717, a time when Naval pensioners received an allowance in beer. Another place to savour Hook's porters and pale ales is Meantime's own stone-flagged, TV-free **Greenwich Union** *(56 Royal Hill; 020 8692 6258)*.

There's a growing market for handcrafted ales, and pubs to meet the demand. **The Market Porter**, opposite Borough Market, showcases up to a dozen unusual microbreweries at a time. **The Old Mitre** in Hatton Garden might be London's most hidden pub (it's between eight and nine, then down an alley) but real ale lovers should already have it on their beerdar. **The Pineapple** in Kentish Town and **The Wenlock Arms** on the edge of Hoxton are also both great places for a proper pint.

Gastro-pubs are a model of convenience we're happy to embrace, combining the atmosphere of pub and eatery and sparing us the temptation of a late-night kebab on the way home. **The Eagle** in Farringdon is regarded as London's original but if you don't mind waiting in the bar for a table (oh, twist our arm) at the no-reservations **Anchor and Hope** on The Cut in Waterloo, there's no better gastro-pub in the city, in our opinion. Dishes are designed to be shared in the low-lit dining room. ◄

touch

THINGS THAT FEEL GOOD

> **TO ENJOY LIFE WE MUST TOUCH MUCH OF IT LIGHTLY.**
> Voltaire

Touch is the first sense we experience and the last we lose. It's how we find our place in the world and relate to everything in it. Touch can be as formal as a handshake with your bank manager or as intimate as a lover's embrace. But in both cases it establishes (almost) the same thing: trust. Touching and being touched can comfort and reassure – it releases antidepressants that can lift moods, calm anxieties, lower blood pressure and even strengthen the immune system.

Isn't it strange then that we spend much of our lives with our hands in our pockets, touchy about the whole idea of touch?

That London Feel

If we open ourselves up to it, everywhere in the city there are opportunities to reach out and touch. Connection with the world around us, whether tactile or emotional, is the most intimate way of getting to know someone, something or someplace.

NATURAL Whether it's your own tactile tour or simply a fleeting moment of contact, nature can soothe and succour us as we make our way through this modern city.

If you're not afraid of people thinking you're a little touched yourself, go out and hug a tree. Explore its texture and character: is the bark young and supple or weathered and wise? Are the wooded roots exposed or self-consciously hidden?

With eyes closed you could tell where and when you are in London by the touch of its trees alone. Rough-barked plane trees place you in suburban streets. Silver birches, smooth to the touch or crunchy between your fingers, mark out seasonal changes in the Royal Parks. Each garden has its own drifts of autumn leaves, like the unusual palette of oaks, cypress and sorbus in Battersea Park; kick through their dried mass, watching them swirl about your legs as the wind dances around you. Flaky yew trees are common in graveyards next to the cool and reflective granite of headstones, and there's no better place to connect with the natural passage of time.

Feel your way around the season's harvest at farmers' markets, comparing earthy, squidgy fungi with smooth, hard squashes. Prodding and sniffing fruit and vegetables is an instinctive way of judging ripeness. Even

Right Here, Write Now

Once in a while detach from the keyboard of your phone or computer (see A Day Disconnected, p 154), and experience the old-fashioned and sensory pleasure of penning a letter to someone you miss who no longer lives in London. Indulge the sense of touch as well as the emotional connection of *staying* in touch.

Savour the scratch of the pen across an uncoated page, and note how every character seems more meaningful when you can't instantly delete. Embellish the page in a way you can't on screen, with a doodle or decoration. Maybe include a newspaper clipping or 'thing' from your life. Head to your nearest post box – no, not a slit in a wall but a proper, red post box, a pillar of communication through war and peace. With the cool, worn touch of the iron and the soft 'ffft' when your letter hits the pile inside, you can't help but feel connected as you imagine your friend's delight when opening the post and finding more than the usual admonishing notices and marketing guff.

at the fishmonger's and butcher's counters, touch can tell us a lot about the produce; fresh fish are firm to a prod while a well-hung steak should retain a finger's imprint. Whether the stallholder will let you poke his produce is another matter.

Avoid the problem by growing your own. Explore seed casings, from hard, shiny rounds ones you can roll between your fingertips like tiny ballbearings to large beans and bulbs. Pot a few wrinkle-seeded peas or tease the dirt off the young roots of a sapling. Prune back brittle, dead wood from fruit trees in February, comparing its dryness with the tender new shoots springing through. Pick the juiciest blackberries you can find, but mind the prickles.

Dig your fingers into some soil as it warms to the touch in March (a sure sign it's ready for new season's spuds) – it's a fantastic way to consign the winter months to the past and, like wearing woollen gloves, it's a way to remind ourselves that everything we depend on – warmth, food, shelter – comes from the land.

Where living objects tell of nature's character, the elements tell of her mood. Soak up sunshine at every chance (through a shirt and smothered in sunscreen, of course). Relish the battering of wind against your cheeks or messing up your hair. On those rare white winter days, throw snowballs until your fingers freeze, then feel the burn of them thawing out in front of a crackling pub fire. And every now and then, submit to the rain; nothing cleanses the mind and soul like standing out in the middle of a downpour.

One of your authors found herself on a typical tactile adventure (when she wasn't even supposed to be doing this chapter!) while wandering through Morden Hall Park in late summer:

'An irresistible giant oak launched me into the tour: its trunk had branched into two, one half showing off familiar rough bark, the other cloaked shyly behind dried, wooded vines. Like light and dark, the tree had formed a perfect dichotomy of texture. This set me off, barefoot on the dewy grass under the full force of the sun. And then the romanticised blether ended with a warm, clumsy splash: a misjudged leap across a shallow stream.

'So I put my shoes back on, and the gravel path crunched underfoot while nettles encroached the walkway and threatened to sting. I kicked open a conker, let its smooth surface polish my palm, and carried it with me to a wilder patch of park. The air became more damp, cooled by a thick canopy of trees, their roots scrambling across the dusty path and prodding my feet as I walked. I couldn't resist putting my boot through the first crunchy leaves of autumn and, er, stubbing my toe on said tree roots.

'A fallen tree became an, admittedly slightly lumpy, bench but it did the job as I watched a duck dart and dive in the river and wondered what it must feel like to skim water. My attention drifted to a tree that had been allowed to die naturally, a rare thing these days as we race to tidy things up and prevent any possible hazards (the nooks and knots are perfect for nesting owls and woodpeckers, apparently).

'I crossed a makeshift wooden bridge, which wobbled unsteadily til I reached the other side, where I found much less. Or much more: a completely different feeling, the lack of touch and the exhilarating freedom of open space.'

CONSTRUCTED If it's lucky to touch wood, our churches and pubs are blessed places indeed. A smooth, polished feel dominates the ancient hardwood pews of St Paul's, while the battered timber bars of our old pubs are equally sacred. Almost 300 years ago, the hands of Britain's most celebrated carver, Grinling Gibbons, crafted the intricate limewood altar surround in the church of St James in Piccadilly and the unique font, supported by Adam and Eve. Running your hand over the beautiful vines today is to connect with both a time and a tradition.

Metal can feel colder but it's an equally good conductor of memories and stories. In places like the National Gallery and the Royal Courts of Justice, the banisters and handrails have been burnished by countless palms. Running soft hands along the worn railings is a timely illustration of how billions of tiny actions can have an effect on something as hard and intractable as metal or stone – a thought that might inspire us when we wonder how to live more sustainably. A similar feeling comes from treading on uneven pavements and staircases that have been worn down by the footfall of generations. At least once, treat yourself to a little DIY reflexology by baring your soles on the rough-hewn cobblestones around London Bridge, the gravelly Thames Path or the worn timber of the Embankment's docks (and then scrub thoroughly!).

In Battersea Park stand the most tactile stones in London: the rounded form of the Barbara Hepworth sculpture and Henry Moore's curvaceous *Three Standing Figures*. Ooh er! For a more bracing touch of stone, join the summer crowds – a surprisingly reassuring experience on occasion – at the Diana Memorial Fountain in Hyde Park, splashing through the eddies and over the cold granite to get to the centre.

But touch isn't just about the soft and yielding pleasures of skin. The most abrasive textures can compel us to satisfy an oft-regrettable curiosity (cactus anyone?). In 2008 artist Roger Hiorns pumped an abandoned bedsit in Elephant and Castle full of copper sulphate solution, which encrusted every inch of the flat in chunky blue crystals. Visitors to the artwork, named *Seizure,* were issued with rubber gloves and boots because the crystals were highly toxic. It's an interesting idea: how to fight the urge to touch something we know we shouldn't.

The Laying on of Hands

Because this is London, there's always a macabre story somewhere; this one (not particularly slow but interesting nonetheless) starts and ends at one of London's gallows. For crimes ranging from theft and arson to murder, prisoners were hanged at Tyburn (which is thought to be just off Connaught Square) and other sites from the 12th century. But their ordeal wasn't over once they had choked; the still-warm touch of a dead person was thought to cure all sorts of ailments so there was often a scrum of people fighting to get a touch of the body. The severed hands of the hanged would change hands for 10 guineas.

touch...

The Cuddle Party

It's a bright Sunday afternoon in north London and I'm in my pyjamas, reclining in a cushion-strewn room among a sprawling pile of 20 people I met just an hour ago. Bob Marley plays softly, massages are given, limbs caressed. This isn't the opening scene in my fledgling porn script; it's one of Britain's first 'cuddle parties' *(www.cuddleparty.com)*.

The idea is simple: in our fast-paced world, increasingly lacking in intimacy and physical affection, these events reintroduce us to the uncomplicated, healing power of human touch. Between 10 and 20 participants or 'cuddle monsters' gather under the watchful eye of a 'cuddle lifeguard' to hug and stroke each other. Pyjamas stay on at all times, you may only touch another 'cuddle monster' if they've given verbal consent and there's a clear sexual line which can't be crossed.

My eclectic but reassuringly normal cluster of 'cuddle monsters' ranges in age from Demelza, a 22-year-old Australian nanny to Maria, a fifty-something from the Caribbean. Then there's Andy, a 26-year-old teacher facing some personal demons. 'I'm terrified of touching people, so I've come to try and get over it,' he says at arm's length. Talk about throwing yourself into the deep end.

'Human touch is a powerful force: it's the first sense we develop in the womb,' says Dr Elvidina Adamson-Macedo, a perinatal psychologist at the University of Wolverhampton. 'The problem now is people feel afraid of touching, because of interpretations of that touch. But you can be very affectionate without being sexual.'

So, how can we remedy our touch deficit? 'Learn to meet and greet more – acknowledge colleagues properly with a handshake,' says Patti Wood, a non-verbal communication expert. 'This creates a positive chemical reaction and helps you feel more positive and connected. If you feel uncomfortable, touch lightly in the safe zone,' says Wood. 'That's anywhere between someone's fingertips and their elbow.'

Then, of course, there are cuddle parties. After a sceptical start I quickly became inhibition-free, embracing men and women indiscriminately. I found myself in a 'half-pretzel' squeeze with 26-year-old Launa, having my hand massaged by a South African actress named Samantha, while my head was being stroked by someone who's name I never even got. The grand finale was a giant 'puppy pile'. And there, at the bottom, his face gleefully poking out from the melee, was haptophobic Andy. His fears quite literally crushed, he emerged from the tangle, excitedly describing himself as 'high on cuddles'.

Jonathan Thompson

Keeping in Touch

A third of Britons live alone, and with email, Facebook and the increasing popularity of virtual worlds like Second Life, we seem to be getting more familiar with internet connections than we are with human relations. It's a paradox of modern life that in a place like London, with so many cohabiting at such close quarters, isolation is perhaps the greatest malaise. The best way to heal urban fractures is to connect with the wider community, the people who live and work around us, by engaging with heads, hands and heart.

VOLUNTEERING Whether it's volunteering for a charity, getting involved with a local school or community group, or simply helping out a neighbour, a little dose of altruism provides a natural high. Even if you can only commit a few hours a week, you'll find there's no shortage of local organisations in need of a hand.

Don't be afraid to be picky; choose something that suits your talents and temperament, something you'll enjoy doing and which will make you feel like you're making a difference. We'll admit also to liking the selfish rewards of selflessness: you'll gain perspective, peace of mind and maybe even a little self-esteem. As philosopher Ralph Waldo Emerson put it, 'no man can help another without helping himself'.

The majority of Britons are concerned that 'we are turning into an urbanised, work-obsessed nation of out-of-town supermarket shoppers', reckon the **Community Service Volunteers** *(www.csv.org.uk)*, a non-profit organisation that has been matching altruistic souls with local organisations since the 1960s. Their annual Make a Difference Day is the easiest way to connect with like-minded people in the community and give something back to the area you live in.

Greater London Volunteering *(www.glv. org.uk)* is another great network if you've got something to give put don't know where to direct it.

Get to know your older neighbours, people who might appreciate someone looking out for them during cold weather. **Neighbours' Day** *(www.european-neighbours-day.com)* is as simple as it sounds: organise a garden tea or street party and get to know the people who live around you. It takes place on the last Tuesday of May, and in one afternoon you can forge connections that might make all the difference to the lonely. **Help the Aged** *(www. helptheaged.org.uk)* partners volunteers with people who could use a friend, someone to help out with the shopping or give them a lift someplace.

The Sock Mob *(homeless.meetup.com/61)* is an ad-hoc, agenda-free group of people who meet and engage with homeless people in London through the simple gesture of offering a free pair of socks. Naturally, that's just an icebreaker; real warmth follows in the connection and conversation. **Carrot mobbing** *(www.carrotmobuk.org)* is a form of social payback where a group of people descend en masse on a business with ethical or environmental polices that deserve to be rewarded with a boost of custom. It's the opposite of a boycott – like dangling a carrot to entice positive action, rather than chastising bad with a boot up the rear. Of course, as slow consumers we do this instinctively, but the idea is that as an international movement the good vibes can gather greater momentum. These things sound intuitive – because they are.

COMMUNITY 'One of the things that slows people down is human relationships,' Carl Honoré tells us over a coffee. 'We try to accelerate everything nowadays – we have speed dating, speed networking – but human relationships have a natural arc. You can't make someone fall in love with you faster. You can't force a friendship. Relationships act like a brake on us.'

A desire to feel like a proper neighbourhood again – you know, playing in the streets, borrowing a cup of sugar – inspired the residents of Hastings, Hartington, Broughton, Denmark and Arden Roads in West Ealing to form the **Five Roads Home Zone** *(www. fiveroadsforum.org)*. A Home Zone is a neighbourhood where the power has been taken away from vehicles and returned to the local residents, to improve safety, encourage neighbourliness and promote sustainability. It began with lower driving speeds, off-road parking and more people-friendly street environments.

But beyond these practicalities, according to Chair Lisa Hall, it's about encouraging community spirit. At the launch tea party, someone asked where all the children riding bikes and playing games in the closed streets had come from: they all lived in the neighbourhood but had been invisible until then.

Older people too are helped to feel less isolated in such community-friendly projects.

Beddington Zero Energy Development or **BedZED** *(www.bioregional.com)* is an optimistic vision of sustainable living, a community of 100 of the greenest homes in London, cottage industries, a car club and an organic city farm ensuring the residents are self-sufficient-ish.

The terraces of Tellytubby-style housing are in Wallington on the outskirts of Croydon, residents pay a fraction of the fuel bills the rest of us do, while community-driven projects such as composting, car-sharing and lavender farming (it gets turned into essential oil) all help people in BedZED get to know each other. You don't have to be a muesli-munching eco-worrier to live there but you might meet a few. The pace of life is definitely slower, not least because cars are discouraged, and some things you just can't hurry, like the compost.

GARDENS Community gardens – and all the joy, fun and focus they bring to their local neighbourhoods – offer a roots-and-all way of getting in touch with your patch. Many are buzzing social hubs, bringing like-minded locals together to laugh, cultivate and maybe even grow themselves, without boundaries of class, wealth, education, race or age. You can even grow veggies.

Countless community gardens have sprouted across London in recent years, as more people dig in against the increasing detachment of city life. The **Federation of City Farms and Community Gardens** *(FCFCG; www.farmgarden.org.uk)* will point you to a local plot, or you can log onto the forum at www.landshare.net. Many are springing up

touch...

from formerly derelict sites, like **King Henry's Walk** in Dalston *(www.khwgarden.org.uk)*, and the award-winning, organic **Culpeper Community Garden** in Islington *(1 Cloudseley Rd; www.culpeper.org.uk)*, which has transformed a corner of rubbish-strewn wasteland into a colourful oasis of flowers, fruit and vegetables, managed by and for local people.

The **Sunnyside Community Garden** *(Hazellville Rd; 020 7272 3522; www.sunnyside.org.uk)* aims to provide horticultural therapy to people with mental and physical disabilities. They're high on sustainability, but low on volunteers, so give them a call.

In 2009 the **National Trust** *(www.nationaltrust.org.uk)* began giving over plots of land for allotments all over the country. The land is on former kitchen gardens, next to or on National Trust properties or on agricultural land. It has even turned the back garden of the National Trust's head office in Queen Anne's Gate into an allotment for staff.

On London's northeastern fringe, in the Lea Valley, is a little place called **Organiclea** *(020 8558 6880; www.organiclea.org.uk)*. It's essentially a community allotment for growing organic, local produce but really resonates as a co-operative and social network. Rather than dividing the garden into separate plots, the whole space is open and volunteers share the work as well as the fruits of their labour. Surplus is sold at market stalls, with subsidies provided to low-income families. Permaculture, a way of cultivating in harmony with nature, is the guiding principle and bike trailers are the main form of haulage. Volunteers also cycle around town foraging for fruit and turning it into jam or juice that's, yep, shared among members. Get a taste of the good vibes at the Saturday market, cafe or organic gardening school.

Guerilla Gardening

Many roundabouts, traffic islands and other utilitarian urban features have had a colourful makeover in recent years, thanks to one man and his merry band of guerrilla gardeners *(www.guerrillagardening.org)*. By day Richard Reynolds is a mild-mannered, thirty-something office worker but at night he scours the streets looking for dead spaces to revitalise.

Armed with little more than a trusty trowel and some seeds, Reynolds has encouraged an army of green-fingered urbanites to reclaim their neighbourhoods with a view to prettying them up for all. Volunteers are assigned troop numbers to preserve anonymity (as they don't always have the full support of councils or the police) and London's various squadrons of guerrilla gardeners have had considerable successes.

They've planted sunflowers opposite the Houses of Parliament, for example, cleaned up one of the ugliest roundabouts in the country (in Elephant and Castle, where Reynolds lives) and since 1996 have harvested lavender from two traffic islands in central London. As well as beautifying the urban landscape, guerrilla gardeners say taking an interest in their surroundings has also provided them with a sort of social therapy.

Using the Plot

When my boyfriend and I moved into a flat in Brixton with a bare concrete balcony just about big enough to accommodate the two of us, I was a 30-year-old Londoner who had never been in possession of any outside space, ever. But once we started decking out our petite eyrie with climbers and hanging baskets, our gardening ambitions grew larger than this small spot would allow. We needed a patch of earth of our own.

The Grove allotments were a half an hour walk away in Dulwich. We toured them on a foggy November afternoon and, rather than being put off by the muddy silhouettes toiling in the cold earth, we put our names down. Six months later we got the call, a half plot (about 30ft by 16ft) had come up. I was full of optimism; it was already May but we could buy some seedlings, get some courgettes and tomatoes in the ground and be eating our own produce by the end of the summer. How wrong I was...

The kind of plots that come up (and are offered to outsiders) are not often the sort that have been lovingly nurtured by their previous owners, weed-free with loamy soil, sunny and just next to a water supply. Rather, like our new rectangle of land, they have been neglected, even abused. Ours had been sowed with grass seed to make a pleasant environment for barbecues and children to play on while their parents worked on the adjacent half that they had actually cultivated. This type of behaviour had been overlooked in the old days ex-plained John, the allotment manager, a man in braces with thick fingers as grubby and gnarled as parsnips. Back then, few people were interested in growing their own. But now allotments are popular, fashionable even; the waiting lists are getting longer, and every scrap of land has to be used.

John sold us a secondhand spade and fork and gave us a piece of advice: 'Don't try and do it all in one day, you'll break your back and never be back. I've seen it happen...' And so, over the next months we came every weekend and spent a few hours turning the earth over, burying the couch grass under an unyielding clay that would harden in the sun and have to be smashed with the back of a spade.

But I didn't mind the work, the blisters and the spider bites, because more often than not the sun was shining and my physical labour had immediate results. We would bring sandwiches wrapped in foil and flasks of tea. We saw toads, butterflies and birds that would feed on the uncovered worms. The traffic, the concrete and the pace of London all seemed to recede and eventually we had a bed that was fit for the three tomato seedlings our neighbour had donated.

The other allotmenteers ranged from young couples like ourselves, trying it out for the first time, to accomplished gardeners who had been there over 30 years, like Peter, the Irishman who cultivated the plot next to ours and would give us bunches of fat salad onions, or Audley from the Carribean, who left little bags of fresh garlic in our com-

ZAI PLUCKS SOME NOURISHMENT FROM THE ALLOTMENT...

post bin. The old-timers were very free with advice, often helpful but sometimes contradictory. Our plot was unfortunately placed at the very entrance to the allotments, and so our efforts drew commentary from all who passed by. 'If one more person tells me how to plant a potato, I am going to kill them...' raged Mike one evening when our fellow allotmenteers had been bestowing their expertise a bit too freely.

But by the following spring our efforts were rewarded with a tidy plot that was ready to receive all the little seedlings I had been nurturing on our Brixton balcony. I planted peas, potatoes, green beans, garlic, spring onions, strawberries, tomatoes, lettuces, carrots, radishes and beetroots, all of which thrived. I was disappointed by my broad beans, supposedly the easiest vegetable to propagate, but which never materialised. And my glossy sweetcorn, pillaged by the squirrels the moment it was ripe. The borlotti beans, a beautiful creamy colour speckled with crimson flecks, were an unexpected success, as was my invincible cucumber plant, which had looked so scrawny at the start of its life, but which must have produced over 30 perfect cucumbers that summer. Peppers and aubergine were over-ambitious without a greenhouse, but butternut squashes and pumpkins seemed to love our thick, damp soil. And our courgettes were so prodigious that I invented a new dish, courgette spaghetti, which would inevitably follow a starter of delicious deep-fried courgette flowers, and which we would eat sitting on our now verdant balcony.

Summer is certainly the most pleasant time for allotment activities, involving a bit of weeding, watering and a lot of harvesting. Winters are bleaker, but even a soggy, cold patch can be alluring. One weekend in December Mike dragged me to our allotment with talk of picking parsnips. 'What's this? Look, something strange is buried there,' he said, urging me to get on my knees and investigate. It was a small metal casket, and inside a note that asked, 'will you marry me?' Magically, a bottle of champagne materialised from inside the compost bin. And so we were engaged, our partnership cemented by compost and courgette spaghetti.

Gavanndra Hodge

Hearth and Soil

'In seedtime learn, in harvest teach, in winter enjoy,' wrote William Blake. He appreciated the benefits of gardening in the city: even in the greyest patches, a garden can brighten the mood. We might hanker after an idyllic cottage in the countryside but the reality for many is that we'd miss the city too much, can't afford the space, and might have to make do with a window box to tune into the rhythm of nature.

Make the most of it. You'd be surprised at what you can grow in a box or a big pot: tomatoes on a sunny balcony, peppery rocket by the bunch that replenishes itself after you pluck a few leaves, or even a few spring onions. Gardeners with more adventurous tastes might like to try garlic and chilli.

Just don't bite off more than you can chew. Herbs are great starter plants, instantly rewarding with their scent and flavour, and the hardier ones like rosemary, mint and thyme flourish in boxes. Garden centres will sell seeds or you can buy online from

Jekka McVicar *(www.jekkasherbfarm.com)*, crowned the Queen of Herbs by Jamie Oliver. She sells organic culinary, decorative or medicinal herbs in both plant and seed form. Depending on the space you have, the likes of **Petersham Garden Nurseries** in Richmond *(Petersham Rd; 020 8605 3627; www.petershamnurseries.com)* can get you started on a range of fruits and vegetables, from raspberries to runner beans, dishing out expert advice on what to grow and when (and following it up with platefuls of inspiration at the cafe afterwards).

If your passion outgrows your windowbox – and an allotment is too big a commitment or too far from home – there are several organisations supporting urban food-growing communities. In south London, **Food Up Front** *(www.foodupfront.org)* provides starter kits with containers, organic compost, seeds and a guide to sowing your first crops. 'Front gardens, balconies and windowsills are valuable areas of land that provide a substantial yield of nutritious vegetables, herbs and salads,' they proclaim; for co-founder Sebastian Mayfield it's about re-connecting city-dwellers with food and enhancing the urban environment. In north London, **Growing Communities** *(61 Leswin Rd, Stoke Newington; www.growingcommunities.org.uk)* planted its first plot in 1996 and has evolved to manage three small, city-centre market gardens. Volunteers of all levels of experience can join in and get their hands dirty, and produce is sold at a weekly farmers' market and through a vegetable box scheme.

Of course, the ultimate reward is cooking with the fruits and vegetables of your labour and sharing it with friends and family. Lately, we've been reviving old family staples that somehow seeped into the subconscious and have been waiting patiently: poached fish on a Friday with hand-cut chips, homemade pies with flaky pastry and parsley liquor, foraged blackberry and apple tarts baked on Saturday evenings, jams and chutneys that make perfect thank-you gifts. It's also nourishing for the soul to realise that this family heritage hasn't been lost by the generation of the convenience meal. ᛘ

...WHILE HIS BROTHER BEN SHOWS OFF THE FRUITS OF THEIR LABOUR

DO

IN THE PURSUIT OF SLOW

NURTURE

MOTION

TRAVEL

SMALL

GATHER

nurture

TAKE CARE OF YOURSELF

> **LET YOUR BOAT OF LIFE BE LIGHT, PACKED WITH ONLY WHAT YOU NEED – A HOMELY HOME AND SIMPLE PLEASURES, ONE OR TWO FRIENDS WORTH THE NAME, SOMEONE TO LOVE AND SOMEONE TO LOVE YOU, A CAT, A DOG AND A PIPE OR TWO, ENOUGH TO EAT AND WEAR, AND A LITTLE MORE THAN ENOUGH TO DRINK; FOR THIRST IS A DANGEROUS THING.**
>
> Jerome K. Jerome

Life is complicated enough without lugging around unnecessary baggage. After all, happiness isn't about what we have, but what we enjoy. Striving for love, health and a homely home is a simple enough goal, or at least one would have thought. But we tend to get distracted by other people's ambitions, the grind of modern life, the race to get ahead or just a struggle to get by. We become so preoccupied with paving our future, we forget to tread joyfully on the now.

It doesn't matter where we seek satisfaction and solace, whether it's in a church, spa, salon, park, cookery class or while collecting daffodils, growing veggies, swimming outdoors, making soap, painting nudes or indeed painting nude. We just need to take it where and when we can. Don't wait to *find* the time or you never will. *Make* the time to nurture your mind, body and spirit and you'll find you can accomplish much more, thus magically creating more time.

Body

Business has been booming in holistic therapies in recent years, as the grapevine resonates with stories of unconventional success, and complementary medicine becomes accepted, even welcomed, by Western doctors. It's only natural, says David, owner of **Luminescents** *(Unit 15, The 1929 Shop, Merton Abbey Mills; www.luminescents.co.uk)*, perhaps the most down-to-earth herb and aromatherapy dispensary in London. 'Most modern pharmaceuticals owe their very development to natural products and ages-old folklore.'

Of course, taking care of oneself requires more than moving from an apothecary to a yoga mat, but it's a jolly good start to self-prescribed TLC.

SPAS AND TREATMENTS

In typical fashion, London has adopted a quick-fix solution to stress. Spas sell us images of tranquil souls in plush white robes being treated to organic facials, seasonal pedicures or even being scrubbed with sapphires – suddenly massage tables and salon chairs seemed like the only place to unwind. It's nonsense, of course, but they are a good way to gift-wrap some time out.

In 1985 a German couple left smoggy Europe seeking a quiet, unpolluted place to grow their flowers and herbs. They settled on organic, biodynamic farms in Australia's sun-drenched Adelaide Hills, founding Jurlique, which they claim is 'the purest skincare on earth', drawing on the ancient art of aromatherapy. Thirteen years later, Londoners Nick and Sue Pierce caught the scent and opened the **Jurlique Health and Wellness Centre** *(300-302 Chiswick High Rd; 020 8995 2293; www.apotheke20-20. co.uk)*, a natural medicine pharmacy, clinic and day spa in one heavenly, holistic centre.

Across the other side of the city and scale, **Spa London** *(York Hall Leisure Centre, Old Ford Rd; 020 8709 5845; www.spa-london.org)* is Britain's first public sector spa. Located in Bethnal Green's historic York Hall, a council-run facility best known as a venue for boxing matches, the spa is set around six heated chambers: you can take a hammam, a Turkish bath, a sauna or a session in the steam room and, if you're brave, follow it with an invigorating ice fountain. There's also a day spa offering massages and treatments at, for London, reasonable prices.

For something a little more exotic, **The Sanctuary** *(12 Floral St; 0870 770 3350; www.thesanctary.co.uk)* is a longstanding women-only day spa in Covent Garden, which draws its signature treatments from across the world. The Sento detox, for example, begins with a Japanese-style bath followed by an exfoliation and Japanese pressure-point massage.

If you're worried about the pampering profession taking itself too seriously, try **Cowshed** *(31 Foubert's Pl; 020 7534 0870, www.cowshedonline.com)*, a laidback shop and spa that sources organic, fair-trade and veggie-friendly botanicals for products such as Dirty Cow handwash or Grumpy Cow uplifting body lotion. Treatments range from the half-day Udderly Gorgeous deluxe maternity pamper, to a quick buff and polish of hands and feet while you sip on green tea.

Men can head across to **Gentleman's Tonic** in Mayfair *(31a Bruton Pl; 020 7297 4343; www.gentlemanstonic.co.uk)* where a wet shave in the traditional barbershop is a luxury to behold. Don't fear, it's not full of colonels having their bushy moustaches trimmed (nor metrosexuals having other areas waxed) – just gentlemen who appreciate the restorative power of a proper shave in an old-fashioned barber's chair, with the possibility of a massage (or even Reiki session) afterwards.

MIND AND MOVEMENT

The ancient martial art **Ta'i Chi** (the 'unstoppable fist') was designed for self-defence, but it's more popularly practised these days to promote health, calm, suppleness and longevity. Early risers will be familiar with the sight of practitioners in public parks; even just watching this beautifully flowing, moving meditation is enough to slow down your heart rate. A variation, known as **Chi Kung**, has been growing momentum lately too (although the movements themselves are incredibly slow). It's a more spiritual approach, literally translated as 'working with the Chi life force'.

If you think these might be your speed, visit www.taichifinder.co.uk for a rundown on the associated benefits as well as a list of classes and the various forms they specialise in. A great way to start the day, and get your mind and body in sync, is to learn a few basic moves and practise them in your favourite outdoor space (or inside and near a window if it's raining).

SWIMMING

Nothing washes away the worries like, as Keats wrote, the 'moving waters at their priestlike task of pure ablution'. Hampstead's poet might have known there is no better spot for wild swimming than the three **Highgate (or Hampstead) Ponds**, off Millfield Lane *(020 7485 4491)*. Regulars have no qualms about a mid-winter plunge before work, but the ponds are much busier on a warm summer's day.

We're spoiled for choice really, with natural pools, manmade lakes and several wonderful art-deco lidos. At the south end of the Heath, **Parliament Hill Lido** *(020 7485 3873; www.camden.gov.uk)* is a good spot for a few meditative laps. Physical activity releases feelgood endorphins and reminds us that London isn't just a place to work. And if we tone in the process, well, who's complaining?

Lidos have been an essential part of the city's summer culture since their 1930s heyday. They're modest places, generally scraping by on community spirit, with the open air and fresh water invigorating every stroke. The newly restored **Brockwell Lido** *(Dulwich Rd; 020 7274 3088; www.brockwell-lido.co.uk)* in south London is a classic example of art-deco design. Over in Hackney, there's the **London Fields Lido** *(London Fields Westside; 020 7254 9038; www.hackney.gov.uk)*, while Hyde Park's **Serpentine Lido** *(020 7706 3422; www.royalparks.gov.uk)* is the venue for a famous Christmas Day swim.

Hardened wild swimmers can also take a bracing dip in the Thames – really! – taking the steps down to the river once used by the **Walton Swimming Club** (the same used by the Thames Valley Skiff Club, off the A3050 at Walton-on-Thames).

Yoga

Blending meditation with varying degrees of physical exertion, yoga is a certain antidote to the accelerated pace of city life and a guaranteed way to switch off. The teacher matters as much as the studio, and we know people who'll cross town to follow a particular instructor. Word of mouth is the most reliable source of information, but if you can't get a personal recommendation, check out the **British Wheel of Yoga** *(www.bwy.org.uk)*, the governing body in the UK, which was set up long before many of us had even heard of Hatha (the most common, gentle and accessible form of yoga, in case you're wondering).

We really like **Laura Watson** *(079 4430 1813; www.yogawellbeing.co.uk)* who runs friendly outdoor classes in Brockwell Park on a Tuesday evening, where people of all ages and abilities stretch against the setting sun to a natural soundtrack of birdsong. There's something encouraging about attempting the tree pose as the wind rustles through the leaves (although the nosey dog-walkers might detract from your confidence). She also runs classes in Regent's Park and in studios across town.

Jeff Phenix *(www.yogajeff.co.uk)* is another widely respected teacher, who hosts classes in varying disciplines at two of the best yoga centres in the city, **Triyoga** in Primrose Hill *(6 Erskine Rd; 020 7483 3344; www.triyoga.co.uk)* and **The Life Centre** in Notting Hill *(15 Edge St; 020 7221 4602; www.thelifecentre.com)*.

Mind

Like a desk piling up with ever-more notes and papers, there's only so much crap the brain can take in before it begins to buckle. Whether we're meditating, reading or learning a new skill, exercising the mind creates clarity, provides perspective and puts us firmly in control.

MEDITATION Nothing empties the mind and soothes the soul like meditation. Whether you're doing a martial art, staring at nature or ideally doing nothing at all, it's the perfect way to clear clutter and cope with stress. We like to think of this whole book as a form of meditation; promoting an everyday mindfulness that helps us celebrate the simple pleasures of London right here and now.

Just like any exercise, meditation gets easier and more beneficial the more you do it, but you might only need a few sessions to build a cocoon you can climb into whenever you need to relax and restore.

On a quiet Victorian street in Kennington stands a solid-looking 19th-century building, the Old Courthouse, the sordid history of crime and punishment of which belies the peace and acceptance that now lies within. The heritage building is the home of the **Jamyang Buddhist Centre** *(43 Renfrew Rd; 020 7820 8787; www.jamyang.co.uk)*, which since 1978 has been providing terrific classes in meditation, Tibetan Buddhism and yoga to stressed out Londoners looking for a slice of inner calm.

Most of the city's best meditation classes draw on the mindful philosophies set out in the Buddhist faith. We also love the **London Buddhist Centre** *(51 Roman Rd, Bethnal Green; 0845 458 4716; www.lbc.org.uk)*, which among other techniques teaches the mindfulness of breathing (who'd have thought it could be so difficult?!). As well as regular classes and lunchtime sessions, they offer restorative retreats to their six-acre patch of sleepy Suffolk.

Kick off your shoes, feel the tickle of the grass underfoot and join the meditation courses held in the gardens at the UK's first Buddhist temple, **Buddhapadipa** *(14 Calonne Rd, Wimbledon; www.buddhapadipa. org)* every weekend during summer. If you're inspired to find out more about Buddhism, there are many other welcoming events held throughout the year.

If you like your meditation without mysticism, try the secular courses at the **London Meditation Centre** *(Notting Hill Gate; 020 7221 0717; www.londonmeditationcentre.com)*, which teach simple ways of stilling the mind.

LIBRARIES 'A room without books is like a body without a soul,' said Londoner G.K. Chesterton. Unlike watching television – a largely passive experience, even when dialling in a vote for *Strictly Come Dancing* – reading a book actively engages the mind, while still letting you zone out in a favourite armchair drinking cups of tea.

London's libraries *(www.londonlibraries. org)* provide sanctuary from the din. At their

Bibliotherapy

With nearly a quarter of million books published here every year, the choice is enough to make your head spin. And if friends and review pages can't be relied upon to steer you in the right direction, you need a bibliotherapist, someone who'll assess your literary preferences and suggest books.

'It's a very personalised service', says Susan Elderkin, who gives bibliotheraphy classes at the School of Life (p153), is an award-winning author of *Sunset Over Chocolate Mountains* (2000) and *The Voices* (2003), and tutor of Creative Writing at Manchester University. 'We help people find their own journeys.' Prescriptions will cover only fiction but if you have a particular problem, such as an impending mid-life crisis or a family member who has fallen out of favour, specific novels can be suggested. I ask about London. I'm a fan of Charles Dickens and Joseph Conrad ('And this also has been one of the dark places of the earth,' says Marlow of London in *Heart of Darkness*) but can Susan suggest some more recent books about the city that I might enjoy? 'Ian Sinclair, who writes about the *East End in White Chappell, Scarlet Tracings*. I think you might also like Ian McEwan's *Saturday*; he's a very considered writer.' Make of that what you will.

Robin Barton

heart, and ours, is the **British Library** *(96 Euston Rd; www.bl.uk)*, 14 floors of fact and fancy that's just the tonic for uninspired city minds: the librarians estimate it would take 80,000 years to work through the whole collection, which contains a copy of every book published in Britain. The reading rooms, with their vaulted ceilings and electrified hush, offer a connection to a weighty, if slightly daunting circle of knowledge.

And then we have humble community libraries, neighbourhood hubs where anybody can breathe in the dusty air of information and imagination accumulating on the shelves. We love the **Carnegie Library** *(188 Herne Hill Rd; 020 7926 6050; www.lambeth.gov.uk)* for opening a Wildlife and Reading Garden in 2007, combining books and birdsong.

Also in south London, **Peckham Library** *(122 Peckham Hill St; 020 7525 2000; www. southwark.gov.uk)*, which won the Stirling Prize for architectural innovation in 2000, has become a local landmark. The building was designed to make people curious about what goes on inside, and seems to have done the trick; events like dance classes and kite making are always packed.

The **Living Library** *(www.living-library. org)* is a little different: instead of books, you borrow a person. The scheme, which began in Scandinavia, is designed to confront prejudice by lending stereotypes (the Muslim, the Immigrant, the Alternative Therapist) to the public for conversation and both parties learn from the experience. The Ex-Gangmember is the most popular person on loan.

CLASS ACTION

Developing or learning a new skill generates energy and enthusiasm and can take you out of yourself (not a bad thing every now and then). From arts to zoology, if any subject has ever tickled your fancy there is probably a course to help you tickle it some more. **Floodlight** *(www.floodlight.co.uk)* will help you find out what's available in your borough. Forget about self-improvement; focus on fun or you'll never get around to it. Here's a prompting guide to get you in the mood.

A place to ponder, **The School of Life** *(70 Marchmont St, Bloomsbury; 020 7833 1010; www.theschooloflife.com)* was founded in 2008 by Sophie Howarth, a former curator at Tate Modern, and offers evening and weekend courses led by some of London's leading lights. You might find yourself on a trip to the Isle of Wight with photographer Martin Parr or discussing travel with philosopher Alain de Botton. At the School's first open day writer James Geary dispensed aphorisms at a table (of London, he said, 'you always see beauty for the first time, ugliness begins where surprise ends.'), while philosopher Julian Baggini served up conversations in the basement. Courses cover work, love, play, politics and the family. Alternatively, dip into one of its Sunday morning 'sermons' at the nearby Horse Hospital, espousing philosophies to live by in a secular age. Slowcoach Tom Hodgkinson delivered the first sermon on Loving Thy Neighbour.

Your work may not end up in a gallery, or even on your own shelf, but creating an *objet d'art* with your own hands can be immensely satisfying. Working with wet clay will help you get in touch with your creative side, and we like the friendly sculpture classes at the

City Lit *(www.citylit.ac.uk)* adult education centre in Covent Garden. In fact, with some 3500 engaging courses here, there's bound to be something to spark interest. If you fancy yourself a little more inventive, the lively short courses at the **Slade School of Art** *(UCL; Gower St; www.ucl.ac.uk/slade)* cover painting, life drawing and even 'drawing as a way of thinking'.

Nowhere do creative, practical and gratifying come together as easily as in the kitchen, and a cooking class is the gift to yourself that will keep on giving. **Sarah Moore's** classes *(www.sarahmoore.co.uk)* go to the heart of slow, inspired by a desire to nourish loved ones with care and consideration. Understanding ingredients is key, she says, and classes focus on seasonality, sustainability and learning to trust your intuition. She also runs tours at Borough and Marylebone Farmers' Market, where she'll introduce you to producers and teach you how to recognise quality, ethically produced ingredients.

Getting down and dirty with nature can be an endless source of slow pleasure. Farms, nurseries and community gardens (see Touch) are the best source of information. **Kew Gardens** *(www.kew.org)* offers terrific short courses and one-off classes in all things natural and seasonal; you might learn how to plant courgettes, photograph trees, or spot hedgehogs' trails in dewy grass.

It sounds corny – and we don't want to create any more wannabe stand-ups at the water cooler – but the **Comedy School** *(15 Gloucester Gate; 020 7486 1844; www.thecomedyschool.com)* helps stimulate personal creativity and works with mainstream and marginal groups to help enhance social skills and even improve literacy.

A Day Disconnected

Studies have found that two-thirds of us actually get anxious if we're separated from our mobile phones. They've become a modern addiction, supported by laptops, netbook, smartphone, iPods, blackberries – the list keeps growing.

Around my desk writhes a tangled viper's nest of cables: power cables, recharging cables, cables to connect my modem to my computer and my computer to my camera. My life can be measured in gigabytes: four gigs of work files, five gigs of photos, 10 gigs of music. I have immediate access to anyone, anywhere, any time. Of course, all this instant information can be wonderful and empowering but when children know more about the Amazonian rainforest than the riverbank down the road, perhaps we're spending too much time glued to screens and not enough in the world around us.

For one day I switched off my mobile phone, logged off my laptop and left my iPod's earpieces unplugged. For the first time I was uncontactable by work, which felt as liberating as streaking along a beach. If I wanted to talk to friends I had to see them face-to-face, and if I wanted to update my blog I had to write my thoughts down in a notebook – how quaint! – and, well, wait. It was a revelation.

I took the bus to the South Bank for a weekly get-together with friends. Without a phone to occupy me, I noticed who got on and who got off, and *wondered* about them. And then I walked down to the river, unhurried, noticing my surroundings as if on holiday. But the greatest difference was having real thinking time. Without skating across oceans of online information I found that concentrating on my own small pool of thought brought more creative ideas.

Slowcoach Carl Honoré tells us he can envisage a future where urban designers create peaceful zones by jamming signals: 'In the 19th century they built green spaces as an escape valve from the grime. I can see a parallel now where you might have technology-free zones where people know they won't be pestered by their phones or other people's shouted conversations. Part of slowing down is knowing when to switch technology off.'

Technology has brought unimaginable advantages and has actually enabled us to live slower lives – by working from home, travelling less for work and more for pleasure, and connecting with people all over the world. But managing the torrent of information, entertainment, opinion, speculation and utter nonsense that floods through our gadgets is a skill lagging way behind the technological thrust. What use is 24/7 access when we're not in a receptive frame of mind to appreciate it? My break from technology did two things; it reminded me how useful technology was and that you could have too much of a good thing. Of course, as someone who never wears a watch, I was also a little late to the pub. And nobody was really fussed. ⚘

Robin Barton

Slow Dates

It's best not to hurry affairs of the heart, which is why slow dates are preferable to shotgun weddings. Where speed dating has all the romance of an auction house, slow dates are about doing something inventive, surprising and wonderful.

The only rule is to keep it simple: you should be breathless with anticipation, not exhaustion. A bit of planning may help, but it shouldn't cost you an arm and a leg.

Fresh air and green spaces 'carry the heart and mind hundreds of miles from the noise and dirt of Cheapside' (to quote a bit of Blanchard Jerrold, if you don't mind). Richmond is a lovers' playground. Indulge in a blanket-in-the-grass picnic and a spot of deer watching before renting a rowing boat from by Old Richmond Bridge. Paddle past Hampton Court Palace and gush at its prettiness, then drift into the bank for a hand-in-hand stroll.

Instead of a quick sandwich, meet for a lunchtime recital at a city church. In winter seek out pubs with open fires, or trade the restaurant reviews for an evening in the kitchen, poking and prodding your way around a market together first. Maybe pick up some seeds or a potted plant because nothing says 'we're in this together' like cultivating new life.

motion

WAYS TO GO

66

SLOW DOWN, YOU MOVE TOO FAST.
YOU GOT TO MAKE THE MORNING LAST.
JUST KICKING DOWN THE COBBLESTONES.
LOOKING FOR FUN AND FEELIN' GROOVY...
LA-LA-LA-LAA-LAA-LAA...FEELIN' GROOVY.

Simon and Garfunkel

99

L ife is indeed a long and winding road. Except these days, it feels like you've got some crazed commuter up your bum, beeping his horn, flashing his lights and making a right nuisance of himself. Go at his pace and you'll miss everything. The journey will be over before you know it, and you won't even remember what it was all about.

You've got two options: risk crashing, or pull over, pause and proceed at your own pace. As important as getting somewhere is, *how* you get there and being master of your own momentum is paramount.

Slow Motion

In the right frame of mind, even the most minor or usually mundane journey can become an adventure. You don't have to go far – just turn right where you usually turn left and see where you end up. In fact, you don't have to go anywhere in particular; it's how you travel that counts. By boat, bike, bus or foot, there are plenty of alternatives to the madness we usually experience when attempting to get around the city.

CYCLING 'The bicycle is the most civilised conveyance known to man,' wrote author Iris Murdoch. 'Other forms of transport grow daily more nightmarish. Only the bicycle remains pure in heart.' What she didn't realise was that cycling would become the quickest way to get around London and an endless source of *schadenfreude* as one glides past stationary traffic.

Nothing opens up the city and creates as close a connection with one's surroundings as a jaunt on a bike; you become part of the scenery and can absorb smells, sounds and sights in an instant. The sensation of freewheeling takes us back to childhood and the sheer joy of self-powered speed. Take solace in swooping detours through parks, cut down mysterious alleys, or just chill out with friends cruising the quieter backstreets.

On a bicycle you're liberated from the confines of a bus, train or car. Cycling takes you places, in your mind as well as a map; it's like entering another dimension, one occasionally punctured by a bit of broken glass or a rough-edged pothole. But even the act of fixing a puncture puts you in the moment and makes you feel like you're at least in control.

Although not particularly cycle-friendly, London is pedalling in the right direction. More than half a million bike journeys are made here daily and the more visible cyclists become on the road, the more cycling facilities will become a priority.

Everyone should try cycling now and then, if only to see how the other half lives (i.e. perilously). If you are not used to life in the bike lane, the **Bikeability** scheme *(www.bikeability.org.uk)* can point you towards a cycle school. Lots of borough councils offer free or subsidised lessons for locals, and **Sunnyside Community Garden** in Islington *(www.sunnysidegarden.org.uk)* offers terrific bicycle maintenance workshops.

Sustainable transport crusaders **Sustrans** *(www.sustrans.org.uk)* reveal routes to rouse the inner explorer: try National Route 4, following the Thames from Hampton Court through Richmond Park and along the South Bank all the way to Greenwich. This is London at its finest: regal, urban, historical and leafy. The various branches of the **London Cycling Campaign** *(www.lcc.org.uk)* post free cycle maps, taking in parks, streets, towpaths as well as parts of the proposed 900km London Cycle Network *(www.londoncyclenetwork.org.uk)*. You'll be familiar with the numbered signs already, which take quieter, low-traffic options where possible. **Transport for London** *(www.tfl.gov.uk)* also gives out cycle maps.

Bike Builders

That favourite of commuters, the humble **Brompton** folding bicycle *(Kew Bridge, Lionel Rd South, Brentford; 020 8232 8484)* is now a London icon – and each one is still handmade in the west London factory. The motivation is simple: freedom and independence of travel, without the constraints of the combustion engine, city planners, the weather, public transport administrators, bike thieves and so on. 'The joy of the Brompton,' explains founder Andrew Ritchie, is that 'though it's become a way of life, I don't have to use it. And when I do, the sense of independence is great.'

Local bike builders go further than the big chains, by handcrafting machines with soul. Witcomb Cycles in Deptford (25 Tanners Hill; 020 8692 1734) has been building frames for 80 years, so it's no wonder they've perfected their steel creations. Down in Croydon, Chas Roberts (89 Gloucester Rd; 020 8684 3370) welds beautiful custom road and mountain bike frames.

A short train trip opens up idyllic countryside for riding, like **Dorking** at the heart of the North Downs for example, which is reached from Victoria, Waterloo or Clapham in under an hour. For ours, the best mountain biking and opportunity to get those endorphins racing is around Leith Hill. Bring a snack and a drink and take it easy once you reach Leith Hill Tower, the highest point in southeast England, taking in the views before weaving your way back down to the station. If that's a little too strenuous head to High Wycombe, just over half an hour from Marylebone, for a cycle ride around the **Chilterns**, an area of chalk hills and streams, beech woodland and relatively quiet roads. Keep an eye out for the distinctive forked tails and scythe-shaped wings of red kites, birds of prey that were re-introduced to this area in the early 90s and are doing rather well.

The ramshackle and community-run **Herne Hill Velodrome** *(Burbage Rd; www.hernehillvelodrome.com)* has been a hotbed of two-wheeled action since it was built in 1891. 'If you turn up on a Saturday morning, you'll see about 50 cyclists of all ages and abilities training on their single-gear bikes,' says local cyclist Mike Higgins. 'They ride in a great pack or in strings of three, four or more, swooping up and down the banks, in and out of each other's slipstreams. The annual, autumn-themed **Ride of the Falling Leaves** departs from here in October, venturing deep into the Kent countryside. A fork in the road offers rather nice symbolism: you can take the long route flat-out with the lycra-clad racers, or choose the less strenuous shorter option that takes in teashops and pubs as you go. You know where we'll be.

WALKING Everywhere is in walking distance, if we take the time. And who's ever regretted taking the time to walk? Strolling clears one's head, stimulates creativity, slows the heart rate and connects us intimately to our little patch of the world. In *The London Perambulator* – perhaps the Slow Guide of 1925 – James Bone dreamed of keys that might unlock the heart of the city, 'her moods and secrets'. Failing such keys, he wrote, 'one must perambulate early and late in all weathers, to know a little about London'.

Some 85 years later, self-described 'ambulatory time traveller' Will Self suggests we have become decoupled from our physical world, and advocates a return to this tradition of the *flâneur* (defined by Baudelaire as 'a person who walks the city in order to experience it'). Indeed, one of the great joys of living in the city is strolling along the South Bank on a summer evening, or dipping into your local neighbourhood at dawn to see who (or what) is up and about. Map the area in your mind as you go, noticing sounds, smells, sights and street names. If you need a little inspiration, there are guided walks covering everything from architecture with the National Trust to wildlife spotting at Hampstead Heath.

Signposted walks can open your eyes to a greener view of the capital. The **Jubilee Walkway** and the **Thames Path** pass through central London, threading together urban oases. A little further afield, the **Green Chain Walk**, laid out in 1977, covers some of the leafiest corners of southeast London. With a couple of hours and a bit of imagination it can transport you between ages, from rollicking parks to quiet cemeteries,

working farms to the 8000-year-old Oxleas Wood, where the wind seems to whisper tales of millennia past through the ancient oak, silver birch, hazel and sweet chestnut trees.

The **Capital Ring** circles the city in 15 sections; a favourite is the route from Wimbledon Park to Richmond Bridge, which starts amid pretty groves around a calm lake, ambling towards the rough glades of Putney Heath and Wimbledon Common. From here it takes in Richmond Park's deer and the Pen Ponds heaving with waterbirds, then passes close to Skye Gyngell's delightful Petersham Garden Nurseries Cafe (p119) for refuelling before opening up to the grand riverside stretch along Richmond Hill for a good old gush.

The London Loop (London Outer Orbital Path) makes a broader circumnavigation of the capital, traversing suburbia and countryside. Dip into sections that prick your interest: the fifth section from Hamsey Green to Banstead is one of the highlights, with a walk along the chalky ridges south of Croydon; or perhaps you'd prefer the towpaths along leg nine from Uxbridge to Moor Park, where trickling water and birdsong drown out the city's stress. All the walks are described on www.tfl.gov.uk and www.walklondon.org.uk, which also provides downloadable audio guides.

If you have a destination in mind and simply want a more gratifying way to get there, check out Jamie Walker's **www.walkit.com**, a website that helps you find the quietest, quickest or least polluted ways from A to B. It will even count the calories you've burned or the CO_2 you've saved, should you be collecting stats, although a true *flâneur* would hardly be bothered with such things.

SHARPLY IN FOCUS, THE NO-LONGER WOBBLY BRIDGE

ON THE WATER

Regent's, Hertford Union and the **Grand Junction Canals** are cleaner than they have been since the Industrial Revolution (read about the returning wildlife in Nature). It's unfailingly therapeutic taking a boat out onto a quiet stretch of water to watch the mist rise over its wake. Swishing along the rivers, tributaries and canals around which the city was built, one can't help but pause and reflect on time and tide. **British Waterways** *(1 Sheldon Square, Paddington; 020 7985 7200; www.britishwaterways.co.uk)* will tell you where you can and can't go.

Little Venice is a great starting point. Sheltered from the surrounding hubbub, the Y-shaped waterway is lined with elegant Georgian villas, and rather more humble homemakers on canal boats. Several operators run trips in restored narrowboats from here (and **Camden Lock**), which pass through London Zoo and Regent's Park. 'Tarporley' *(www.camdencanals.org)* is a 70-year-old narrowboat, which can take you into a secret world, such as through the three-quarter-of-a-mile-long Islington Tunnel on Regent's Canal (which early users would navigate by pushing through the darkness with their legs on the side walls).

The Thames used to be a highway abuzz with tugs, royal barges, police boats and families splashing out on daytrips. Whilst being rowed along the Thames one morning and singing a jaunty tune, Samuel Pepys records how a stranger in another boat joined him singing seconds, and in this oh-so-lovely manner they made their way to Deptford. The streamlined catamaran between the Tates is less lyrical, but gives you a taste of travel on the river, running every 40 minutes when the galleries are open. Official riverboats *(www.tfl.gov.uk)* run regularly from 15 moorings dotted along the river, including Wandsworth, Greenwich, Westminster and Blackfriars. The **River Thames Boat Project** *(www.thamesboatproject.org)* is dedicated to giving older people or those with learning or physical disabilities the chance to take a boat trip on the specially adapted 'Richmond Venturer'.

Self-powered travellers might prefer a sunset or sunrise kayak on the canals with **Thames River Adventures** *(07773 720 860; www.thamesriveradventures.co.uk)* while the **Thames Valley Skiff Club** *(www.tvsc.co.uk)* specialises in traditional, hand-crafted racing boats (the original water taxis) and sailing clubs proliferate around Richmond and down by the Isle of Dogs. The western Thames takes in centuries-old regal views like Syon Park and Hampton Court Palace, but paddling a dinghy in the shadow of Canary Wharf's towers, the derelict warehouses, docks and urban panoramas further east can be just as evocative.

ON THE BUSES

Travelling by bus is to give oneself up to a higher power. Even if you run, there's no guarantee the driver will hold the doors, and you may end up waiting at the stop two minutes or 20. There's no use fretting over traffic or detours – just take in the rolling view, you'll get there when you get there. Relax into the rhythm of it and interact with London. You might even be so daring as to strike up a conversation; 'the man on the Clapham omnibus' can offer a wealth of intrigue. And, of course, the bus will always

Roadworthy

City traffic has all the downsides of slow without any of the benefits – it's stressful, pointless and multifariously taxing. But the car needn't be the nemesis of slow; **Liftshare** *(www.liftshare.com/uk)* does exactly what it says on the tin. Simply sign up and find out who is going where, then hop in for a lift. Letting someone else do the driving for a change is a good way of seeing the city anew, uncovering a new route or even a fresh perspective.

take you back to where you started – eventually – in the circle of city life.

So, jump on a random bus and see where it takes you. **Route 3**, for example, lets you feel like a tourist for a day, minus the camera-toting crowds. Pick it up in Herne Hill, taking in the increasingly ordered streets from Brixton to the Thames, crossing Lambeth Bridge, sidling along past the Houses of Parliament (sit upstairs on the left for a sweeping birds-eye view), before passing the Palace of Westminster, Horse Guards, Trafalgar Square and Piccadilly Circus.

Retired bus driver Denzil 'Scotty' Scott began driving a **Routemaster** in 1970. 'Around Christmas time you used to get so many little gifts and people would always be singing on the bus,' he recalls. Benign and beautiful, old Routemasters had a warm personality that's lost on the angular modern versions with their CCTV pods and advertising screens. If you're missing that wonderful curved ceiling, the 1960s livery and the harmony of their shape, take the 15 or the 9 – making a nostalgic run for the pole at the back. **Route 9** goes from Royal Albert Hall and Aldwych via Trafalgar Square, Piccadilly Circus and Hyde Park Corner. But Scotty prefers the 15, which runs between Tower Hill and Trafalgar Square via St Paul's cathedral.

OVERLAND & UNDERGROUND

At rush hour, from the bridge at Liverpool Street Station, watch commuter ants dashing hither and thither as trains pull in and out. Break ranks: say hello to platform staff, climb the '193 stairs' warned of at Covent Garden, notice the unique tile tessellations at each station or the art under Gloucester Road's brick arches. Allow time to get off a stop early or late, and weave your way to your destination through the streets. On board, use your time creatively (see Work) or notice how the time affects the mood – hardworking to hedonistic, revelling to reflective, the Tube incubates the city's disposition like nowhere else.

Check out the hobbyist **Through the Window** rail guides *(www.railwaybritain.co.uk)* to appreciate the major overland routes out of town. One journey, for example, departs 'Waterloo's curving platforms', rattling parallel to the Thames offering glimpses of the Houses of Parliament, Lambeth Palace and the Battersea Power Station, before passing Wandsworth Common, crossing the River Wandle, and diverting into a cutting that leads to JR Scott's 'magnificent' 1937 Surbiton Station, with its 'art deco clock tower and modernist façade'. ❧

travel

PLACES TO REACH

66 **I TRAVEL NOT TO GO ANYWHERE, BUT TO GO. I TRAVEL FOR TRAVEL'S SAKE. THE GREAT AFFAIR IS TO MOVE.** 99
Robert Louis Stevenson

We've spent plenty of time celebrating the good, slow times to be had in London, but one of the best things about living in the capital of somewhere so beautiful and varied is the opportunity and lure to get out. An hour or two on the train – the time many of us spend commuting each day – can transport us to a different world of natural delights. Ancient tombs, seaside cliffs, bucolic countryside, chalky hills, still winter lakes, university cities and bohemian towns – there seem to be more opportunities for weekends away than there are weekends to actually go away.

Going somewhere new changes our mindset; free of everyday constraints, we seem to create more time to delight in the small and the slow. Every escape from routine is a deliberately slow pursuit, but some, we suggest, are just a little slower than others.

Holiday at Home

Picture your travels in London over the last week. Like the rest of us, you probably took the same routes to the same places on the same days by the same means. Perhaps during your undeviating days you imagined a holiday – after you've cleared this busy period or that debt. But what's stopping you taking a break right now? Block out some slow time on your calendar, 'negotiate' a mental health day from work, or simply spend your lunch hour embracing London as if for the first time.

Turn left where you'd usually turn right and see what you find. Leave buildings by the side door or take a different exit at the station. Follow a ray of light or a stray feather caught in the wind (and if your friends think you're losing your mind assure them that, on the contrary, you're finding it again). Turn off the iPhone, dress down, grow a beard. Check out a big old museum you haven't been to in years, a trendy new gallery or just a neighbourhood you've been meaning to visit.

Even better, jump on a random bus and see where it takes you; if you don't like your destination, it'll return soon enough. Visit a new bar, eavesdrop on the locals and see how the pulse differs from where you live (if, indeed, it does).

Don't be too proud to visit tourist attractions you've been curious about but never actually experienced – they lure visitors from all over the world, don't you know. Carry a camera and take snapshots of the city, or spend an afternoon sketching a familiar view.

Combine the wonder of a tourist with the wisdom of a local: rather than joining the map-wielding crowds, head to Hyde Park at dawn to watch the Household Cavalry limber up, or see them parade under Wellington Arch from your high (and mighty, perhaps?) vantage on the balcony – Life Guards at 10.40am, Blues and Royals an hour later. 'No one's ever here for that,' says James in the ticket office.

Make a whole week of it if you can. 'Staycation' has become a buzzword of the moment (trumped only by its forefather, 'economic downturn'). Think about it: no schlepping to the airport by £25 train or £50 taxi, no queuing to check-in at 6am or shuffling through security with your shoes in one hand and your belt in another. No being charged to take a suitcase with you. No sitting in a cramped seat breathing recycled air for three hours before touching down only to go through the process again in six days.

'Last summer, rather than pack up the car, we just put the TV away, got some different foods in and made up packed lunches,' says Londoner Sophie Brown. 'Then we went and did all the things we'd never got round to before as a family – seeing the penguins being fed at London Zoo, taking a boat trip down the Thames, and, for the boys, a tour of the new Wembley Stadium. It was all in London and it was all fantastic.' 🐎

Time Out

Just trying to *decide* where to spend that precious weekend can makes the holiday seem like hard work. It's a subjective task, too: some may seek Shakespeare and butterflies in Stratford-Upon-Avon, others Victorian seaside amusements in Brighton. Total seclusion at a farmhouse in Dorset, perhaps, or a weekend of croissants and Cézanne in Paris. You may like to contemplate time and nature at Stonehenge, itself built to worship the sun and moon, or you might rather the less charted relics of the Sutton Hoo kingdom.

Thankfully, in a slow frame of mind you can't make a wrong move but here are a few ideas if you need a nudge. We've followed the rattle and clack of train tracks, seeking out spots that seem to carry us furthest from the city without necessarily taking too long to get there.

OXFORD Life is a lot less rushed in Oxford, a city of writers, bicycles and decent pubs. It took JRR Tolkien 10 years to write *Lord of the Rings*, in between pints with CS Lewis at the Eagle and Child on St Giles. It might be just over an hour from Paddington, but it feels like another century (until a cyclist running late for class sends you careening from your reverie). Slip back 800 years as you amble around the honey-coloured colleges like **Balliol** or **Merton**, or the **Radcliffe Camera**, arguably the most beautiful library in Britain, taking time to watch the changing light dappling the golden stone.

In this spacious city, green spaces are as important as seats of learning. Catch a game of cricket in the **Oxford Parks** during summer before following the sound of running water to the river. Look out for the beautiful arched bridge, from where you can see punts negotiating their way up to the **Cherwell Boathouse** *(01865 515978; www.cherwell-boathouse.co.uk)* for a pitcher of Pimm's. Rent your own from the boathouse by Magdalen Bridge at the east side of the city centre, or

find a nearby bench to watch the comedy of splashes and crashes of first-time punters. Crossing the road from Magdalen College, you'll find the delightful riverside **Oxford Botanic Garden** *(01865 286690; www.botanic-garden.ox.ac.uk)*, where time slows in sync with the River Cherwell's eddies.

Our favourite pubs are in the Jericho quarter of the city, to the north of the centre. Cross St Giles and head north until you reach Little Clarendon St, where you can stop at **George & Davis'** *(55 Little Clarendon St; 01865 516652; www.gdcafe.com)* for homemade ice cream and ethically sourced tea and coffee. The area ahead of you is Jericho, home to the grand Oxford University Press and our favourite pub, the **Old Bookbinders** *(17–18 Victor St)*, which has real ales and the sort of faded interior you could settle in for a few hours. The canal borders the west side of Jericho and following it north will lead you to Port Meadow, the city's second great green space. At this northern edge of the city the sky seems to open out onto pastures, towpaths and some of the loveliest B&Bs in town.

CAMBRIDGE

We dare not mention one without the other. Cambridge is smaller than Oxford, but more freethinking, according to our friend Jess. Some mind-bending discoveries (DNA and the evolution of stars, to name a few) seem to give the theory credence.

Life in Cambridge involves sprawling in a gorgeous old quad or lounging by the River Cam under the weeping willows, pondering big thoughts while gorging on Byron and Shelley. You don't have to enrol to do the same, and being only 50 minutes from King's Cross or Liverpool St, there's no reason not to skip up here for a calm, contemplative afternoon.

Unlike Oxford, you can wander through the colleges of compact Cambridge until you find a spot to sit and read that really suits your pace. Jesus has a sombre, ecclesiastical air, while King's has a magnificent, ebullient chapel (with famous choir) that looks out over the Backs, a waterway packed with punts during the summer. Clare is a Renaissance creation, elegant rather than forceful, while small, plain Sidney Sussex appeals to the puritan within (Oliver Cromwell was one of the college's first students). The largest is Trinity, which earns its place in our hearts as home to AA Milne, creator of the slowest character in fiction, Winnie the Pooh.

BRIGHTON

'Brighton's all about fun and frivolity,' says Brighton-born Londoner Ruth, who gave us the inside track. Being the traditional playground of Londoners since the 18th century, you might expect a seaside town overrun with flamboyance. You're only half right; the irrepressibly energy, a combination of culture and seaside winds, is exactly why we love it.

Leave the museums and art galleries, and instead hit the **Lanes**, the funky little shopping area downhill and on the left from the station. It's pedestrians only here so you can check out the boutiques, art shops, vintage stores and cafés in relative peace. Further downhill, beside Pavilion Parade is the cream-coloured **Royal Pavilion**, the famously over-the-top Prince Regent's holiday home, complete with Russian-style domes and minarets. There's a lovely lawn area to stretch out on while you ponder your next move.

On Ruth's advice we crossed North St and went down to the seaside and the Brighton of summer postcards: the sharp smell of fish and chips, sweeter candy floss, deckchairs on the shingle, seagulls dive-bombing tourists, people flirting, laughing, hoping the sun comes out. It's only an hour from London Bridge or Victoria and perfect for a summer skive and seaside dip. Soaring, whitewashed Regency villas and decorative 1920s touches meet the brash, flashing amusement arcades along Palace Pier, adding a final flourish to the festive mood. Watch the world go by with an ice cream – street entertainers, rollerbladers, families at play – letting your mind drift with the gulls.

THE COTSWOLDS

No two locals seem to agree on what a 'Cotswold' actually is, beyond a 'group of hills' – a fitting reflection of characters along this 100-mile range.

Stroud is about 90 minutes from Paddington and a little grittier than the neighbouring towns, but no less beautiful and with a distinct bohemian edge.

Its dramatic landscape insulates a heady creative spirit – this is a town that really seems to belong to its artists. You'll meet them in markets, galleries or just by the lake, absorbed in their sketchbooks. It seems that every beautiful historic building that *can* be turned into a studio has been. There's no point listing them, for the joy is in the wandering, following your whims into this nice old landmark or that cobbled lane, asking a friendly shopkeeper for recommendations or tracing the footsteps of the woman in the blue hat. Along the streets, chalkboards dusted with cursive scrawl advertise painting and sculpture classes, to really draw your mind away from the city. There are also little arty cafes and bookshops, awesome walking trails and, every Saturday, a perfectly idyllic farmers market.

THE EDEN PROJECT

Five hours from 'the big smoke' can take you to South American rainforests or Mediterranean gardens, or at least pockets of each in the biomes – the largest greenhouses in the world – of The Eden Project. Designed to make us more mindful and appreciative of nature, this is a phenomenal feat of eco-friendly architecture built on an exhausted clay quarry. The whole place tells stories that bring nature to life, with staff working overtime to promote clean energy, ecological education and ideas for sustainable living. Lofty aims aside, a visit also offers small pleasures, like seasonal harvest festivals (and indeed delicious food at any time), imaginative play for children, and natural rewards aplenty for those who take the time to smell the wildflowers. In summer, the biomes provide a spectacular backdrop for high-profile gigs known as the Eden sessions.

Surrounding **Cornwall** offers plenty in itself, including miles of walking trails – from wild coastline to sheltered bays, ancient moorland to calm estuaries – to stretch minds and legs. The warmth of the Gulf Stream ensures stunning gardens aplenty (*see www. gardensofcornwall.com*). We also love the restored estate that's ever-so-romantically known as the **Lost Gardens of Heligan** *(Pentewan, St Austell; www.heligan.com)*, where wanderlust is indulged in alpine ravines, banana plantations, carved New Zealand tree ferns, towering tracts of bamboo and dense ancient woodland.

Journey into Space

When you get caught up in thinking the world revolves around you, and terrestrial distractions don't work, take a journey into space. The first time you see the moon through a telescope is unforgettable, exploring its pocked and creviced surface and imagining it controlling the tides, the groundwater table beneath our feet and, perhaps apocryphally, our own moods. Looking into space is a wonderful way to feel small, not a bad thing every now and then. It's also the surest way to burst out of that hazy urban bubble if the seemingly starless sky ever stifles you. **The Royal Observatory** *(020 8858 4422; www.nmm.ac.uk; see p22)* hosts sky watch and planetarium events regularly.

Departures

	Departures	Departures	Departures
res	13 Platform —	1339 Platform —	1348 Platform —
tform —	on	Feversham	Maidstone East
&		Calling at Page 1 of 1	Calling at Page 1 of 1
Page 1 of 1	Page 1 of 1	Bromley South	Bromley South
		St. Mary Cray	Swanley
		Swanley	Otford
		Farningham Road	Kemsing
		Longfield	Borough Green
	nction	Meopham	West Malling
		Sole Street	East Malling
	outh	Rochester	Barming
		Chatham	& Maidstone East
	Hood	Gillingham (Kent)	
	ington	Rainham (Kent)	
		Newington	
		Sittingbourne	
	d Tonbridge	Teynham	
	Southeastern	& Feversham	
		Southeastern	Southeastern

11

⚠ WARNING

Sleepers

If the journey matters as much as the destination, then taking an overnight train to Scotland must surely be one of the slowest getaways of all. Our northern neighbour offers plenty of natural places to take stock, and nothing beats reaching them by languorous sleeper, an infinitely more restful start to a weekend away than the mad dash through Friday afternoon traffic. The rattle of the train through the still, dark night is a lullaby for the ages, rocking you into an unexpectedly deep sleep.

And it's a good thing, too; waking up in **Edinburgh**, you'll want to be refreshed for the steep climb from Waverley Station up to Edinburgh Castle and into the **Old Town** behind it. Explore the independent shops in the lanes winding down to the Grassmarket, before letting your appetite lead the way to **The Outsider** (15–16 George IV Bridge; 0131 226 3131) for a delicious traditional meal for under a fiver (this definitely isn't London): try the ham hock and marrow fat pea ragout, or chicken liver risotto with caramelised onions, walnut and brandy.

Edinburgh's wealthy began moving across to the **New Town** in the 18th century, and the grid of streets are a masterpiece of Georgian town planning, with beautiful three-storey terraces and wide roads. Enjoy the architecture around George St and Charlotte Square before dropping into the **National Gallery of Scotland** (The Mound; 0131 624 6200; www.nationalgalleries.org), where William McTaggart (not to be confused with his grandson MacTaggart) captures some tumultuous Scottish landscapes and seascapes.

Take the sleeper to **Fort William** instead and you'll see the wild landscapes for yourself. Start the morning with a stroll up Britain's highest mountain, **Ben Nevis**, letting the stark mountain air clear the dust from your lungs. The trails are not as tough as they sound, and if you've had enough, you can simply turn around and shift into easy downhill gear. 'Great things are done when men and mountains meet,' wrote William Blake, and the stunning green-on-grey landscape, with the grand thoughts it inspires, seems to prove his words (although to be honest, it's just as enticing to sit back, take it all in and actually *do* nothing). In the town itself, linger over a fresh seafood lunch at **Crannog Restaurant and Smokehouse** (The Pier; 01397 705589; www.oceanandoak.co.uk), situated on the pier overlooking the tranquil waters of Loch Linnhe. From Fort William, a local train offers to take you on one of the most scenic journeys in the country, to the tumbledown fishing port of Mallaig. And from there you could head across to Skye, and then you could skip across the Hebrides…the journey need never end, if only you didn't have to get back to work. ⚓

Trains depart Euston; you'll need to book in advance at www.nationalrail.co.uk

small

SLOW THINGS FOR KIDS

> ## TO SEE A WORLD IN A GRAIN OF SAND, AND A HEAVEN IN A WILD FLOWER, HOLD INFINITY IN THE PALM OF YOUR HAND AND ETERNITY IN AN HOUR.
>
> William Blake, *Auguries of Innocence*

Though they're usually the ones racing around – and at least *perceived* to be the cause of much of our own acceleration – children have a wonderful knack for simplifying life and dragging us over into the slow lane. Remember what it was like to be three feet tall, enthralled by the most commonplace sights? Walls at eye-level beg to be climbed, and keyholes peered through. Upon inspecting a petal, one might discover a ladybird or ant – and weave a whole story around it. You'll be performing a mundane task like putting out the bins, while your kids will be admiring the moon.

Seeing things as a child does goes to the heart of the slow philosophy. Feeling pure and uncomplicated joy, delighting in the small things, being quick to wonder and slow to lose our innocence are all things to which we should aspire. So rather than overanalysing everything, surrender to the instinct and imagination of kids, pick the fuchsia on the way home from school and admire the 'wiggly worms' as you go.

Thrills, Chills and Spills

London is full of stimulating environments to expand the natural curiosity of kids: their determination to suddenly stop and pick up some autumn leaves or dance up the steps of a public building forces us to change our pace, even our objectives – no bad thing every now and then.

HOME But let's start by going nowhere special. Children are the best possible excuse to play and be frivolous. Take time to share their interests and you'll rediscover endless wonders in the back garden, kitchen or in the world of make-believe.

After a week of school, sport, music practice, homework and getting in and out of the car, there's nothing like rushing into the back garden or sprawling on the living room floor and staying put. Bake bread from scratch, or pick wild blackberries and make a deliciously messy pie. Talk Dad into grilling cocktail sausages on the barbeque and eat them with little sticks, the grease running down your wrists and onto the grass. Erect a tent in the back garden, or make your own with sheets over the dining table, and turn it into a yurt by filling it with as many scatter cushions as you can find. Zip yourselves in and tell ghost stories by torchlight, then calm yourselves down by making proper cocoa, stirring it slowly over the stove.

Plant seeds, whether or not you have a garden. In fact, a very enjoyable way to garden is by keeping it small and using a window box or terracotta pot. Vegetables like radishes, lettuce and cherry tomatoes are easy and thrilling to watch grow, or plant some bright eye-catching flowers like sunflowers, marigolds and nasturtiums. Paint a flowerpot, dress yourself in daisy chains, press flowers in a book and make cards with dried petals and leaves.

Take your blanket outside when you first wake up, and wrap up on the dewy grass listening to the birds. Count the different species that visit your garden and get a book from the library to help identify each one. Feed the birds and offer them a shallow tray for a bath, then stand back and admire as they feed and frolic. Start a nature table for found objects like an eggshell, peculiar twig or a nutshell that's been cracked by a squirrel; life cycles have a wonderful way of putting things into perspective.

Kid-friendly Festivals

Imagine, the children's literary festival on the South Bank in February, brings fantasy to life with performances and imaginative workshops based on familiar stories. **The London Children's Film Festival** *(www.barbican.org.uk)* in November features family-friendly films and workshops, while the summer-long **Watch This Space** at the National Theatre has an inclusive array of dance, theatre and music for all ages.

SCOPE FOR THE FUTURE AT THE GREENWICH OBSERVATORY

PARKS AND PLAYGROUNDS

Don't overlook the simple pleasure of a walk through the local park or neighbourhood; kids often require a bit of coaxing, but once they get going they love the chance to dodder and dash. An outing to any half-decent London park (see Nature for a few favourites) can be transformed into something special with a little creative thinking. Make an event of it, with before and after elements that will enrich the experience. A few slow games and activities on the way might be a good idea to keep the kids amused. It could be as simple as some timeless 'I spy' or some questions and riddles that will be answered later when investigating the natural world of the park.

Seasonal trips to the same park open up opportunities to compare how the trees, plants, birds, animals and indeed people change their habits as the natural cycle progresses. See if you can spot a herd of deer at Richmond or Greenwich, rutting during autumn or caring for their young in June. Look out for telltale signs of the different seasons, like acorns, conkers, dry leaves or wildflowers for pressing. 'Plant craft' is a great way to continue the fun at home – you could make a picture frame from twigs, a bird feeder from pinecones or a mobile out of different-coloured autumn leaves.

But the real attraction is simply the opportunity to wander aimlessly for hours through a park's enormous, meandering expanses. Let the kids take the lead and walk, scoot or cycle the random paths that crisscross the grounds. Jump into a pile of leaves gathered up by the wind; stroll through rambling wildflowers and beautifully planted rose gardens and try to smell the difference between the colours; identify the birds you hear by their song and yell out your guesses; climb a big old tree; or just find a grassy hill and tumble down it as fast as you can. Then switch over into wildlife spy mode, treading very softly in the wilder, quieter parts of the parks, looking out for the rare flash of a kingfisher or listening for frogs and different insects.

The outdoors inspires the best fantasy games, providing floral crowns and stick swords aplenty. Invent elaborate stories as you go, maybe using Hyde Park's Upside-down Tree, officially called a weeping beech, for your castle. The **Diana, Princess of Wales Memorial Playground** in Kensington Gardens *(Black Lion Gate, Broad Walk; 020 7298 2141)* has a fantastic wooden pirate ship (parrots not included) plus several teepees and treehouses to use as dens and an area designed for less able-bodied children. This is one of our favourite adventure playgrounds, with wind chimes, aromatic plants and playful sculptures stimulating all the senses.

Indeed, it is healthy for children to experience thrills and spills in a safe environment – in spite of our increasingly risk-averse culture – and adventure playgrounds stretch imaginations as well as smiles. Kids can take a jump on a flying fox at **Coram's Fields** in central London *(93 Guilford St; 020 7837 6138, www.coramsfields.org.uk)*, pet farmyard animals, build sandcastles or feel their way around the sensory play area, all within a stone's throw of the British Museum. The best playgrounds follow the slow principles anyway: they have natural settings, offer sensory activities, are community-run and encourage creativity. The comprehensive www.londonplay.org.uk website will help you find one close to home.

CITY FARMS

Animals bring out the best in kids, and interaction with wild and domestic creatures offers a wonderful big sensory dose of the smelly, living, barking or mewing natural world. Even the most urbanised patches have rural corners, where the rich smell of manure permeates and oinks and bleats drown out sirens and shouting. Most city farms are free and passionately educational. **Mudchute Park and Farm** in the shadow of Canary Wharf on the Isle of Dogs *(Pier St; 020 7515 5901; www.mudchute.org)* is home to more than 200 animals, from cows and sheep to rather more unusual llamas and ferrets. There's always something to do, whether it's taking morning horse-riding lessons at the stables, sharing lunch at the delicious Mudchute Kitchen, or helping round up the Gloucester Old Spot pigs and Pygmy goats half an hour before closing. All this against the backdrop of the tallest towers in the country? Magic.

Another of London's original city farms, **Hackney City Farm** *(1a Goldsmith's Row; 020 7729 6381; www.hackneycityfarm.co.uk)* still does a great job of engaging kids, not only with where their food comes from, but also with why it matters. It has a wide range of animals, from the four rust-coloured Tamworth pigs who arrived in 2008, to Larry the donkey, a local TV celebrity. As well as the regular routines of a farm – growing food, milking cows, keeping bees – this one also organises pottery and upholstery classes.

Just a short walk from the Thames, the animals of **Vauxhall City Farm** *(165 Tyers St; 020 7582 4204; www.vauxhallcityfarm. org)* are perhaps the closest to the seat of power in Westminster (insert your own *Animal Farm* joke here). This happy, noisy place is the full sensory shebang: there are music and movement classes for under-5s, while spinning and weaving programmes make use of the farm's dye garden and wool from its sheep. It's also home to a fantastic Riding Therapy Centre, which works with disabled and disadvantaged children to reduce stress and boost confidence.

MUSEUMS AND GALLERIES

Although rarely top of a child's to-do list, museums and galleries are outdoing each other these days to entertain kids who'll love their visit as long as it's kept entertaining, lively and short. An even surer bet are activities, events and courses offered during the summer holidays and on weekends throughout the year. A series of family trails wind around the **British Museum** *(Great Russell St; www. britishmuseum.co.uk)*, following themes like hunting for dragons. There are also free activity backpacks and art materials (crayons are to be kept well away from the priceless exhibits!). And as with all museums, take an audio guide whenever it's offered; kids love the independence of wandering at their own pace, being directly addressed by the guide and, of course, pressing all the buttons.

The trio of museums in South Kensington have outstanding programmes of activities for children. Best of the bunch is probably the **Science Museum** *(Exhibition Rd; www. sciencemuseum.org.uk)* where exhibitions are designed to provoke – and thankfully sate – young curiosity. There are also special events such as overnight sleepovers, which make science so appealing that you'll need to book well in advance.

Over at **Greenwich**, the National Maritime Museum, the Royal Observatory and the Planetarium are magnets for star-struck kids. The questions here inspire young and old alike. What is time? What's in space? Where do we fit in? Tuesdays are a family play day at the NMM for under-5s, while Sundays have a whole range of activities (making sea monster costumes is always a favourite). There are also special shows for children at the Planetarium at weekends.

There are workshops and storytelling sessions at the **National Gallery** every Sunday for families, plus two-day workshops led by established artists for 12–17 year olds in the gallery's own studios. At **Tate Modern**, ask for the Start game, which will guide you around the gallery doing special tasks. Tate Britain's special events for youngsters are decided by the Tate Forum, a group of people aged from 14 to 25. There are also some fantastic activities inspired by the works in the gallery, such as making outfits to resemble those in paintings. The **Design Museum** runs Sunday afternoon workshops with month-long themes in their child-friendly design studio overlooking the Thames. Design a model car, become a fashion-obsessed milliner: whatever the task, the tutors are experts at tailoring it for kids.

CLASSES AND ACTIVITES

Booking kids up for out-of-school activities needn't turn them into over-timetabled, clock-watching mini-employees; rather, a few slow interests can ignite ideas and dreams they'll want to explore in their own time. The trick is in keeping it local, saving on travel time and fostering new friendships in the neighbourhood. Merely as a primer, here are a few of our favourites across the city.

Drama Queens and Kings: Wimbledon's much-loved **Polka Theatre** *(240 The Broadway; 020 8543 4888; www.polkatheatre.com)* delights in stirring emotions, sparking the imagination and encouraging children to develop creatively. There's a strong professionalism to the teaching and productions, but kids will be having far too much fun to notice.

Sound of Music: **Wigmore Hall** in the West End *(36 Wigmore St; 020 7258 8200; www.wigmore-hall.org.uk)*, one of Europe's finest classical music venues, also takes an active role in introducing young people to chamber music and song. The six month-long Chamber Tots course nurtures children aged two to five through live music-making and a short concert. Don't be intimidated by the talent: it all comes from the heart.

Art Lovers: **The Dulwich Picture Gallery** *(Gallery Rd; 020 8693 5254; www.dulwichpicturegallery.org.uk)* hosts workshops and courses throughout the year. The Saturday Art Extravaganza for 7–10 year olds includes felt-making and T-shirt design. For 11–14 year olds there are silkscreen printing and drawing classes, while older children can build a portfolio with proper studio time and a life model, all under expert tuition in one of London's most pleasant galleries.

Action Heroes: Learn to jump through hoops and other tricks at the **Circus Space** *(Coronet St; 020 7729 9522; www.thecircusspace.co.uk)*. Courses for 8–18 year olds run for 12 weeks and include trapeze, juggling, tight-wire and storytelling. You might be relieved to know that lion-taming is not part of the curriculum.

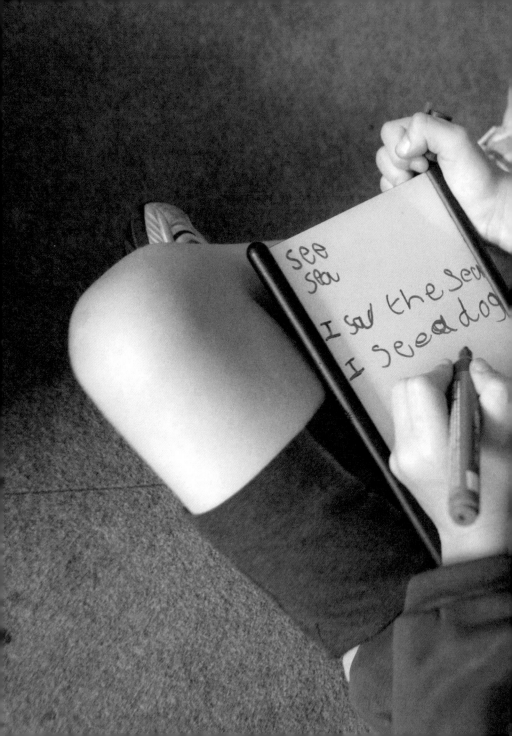

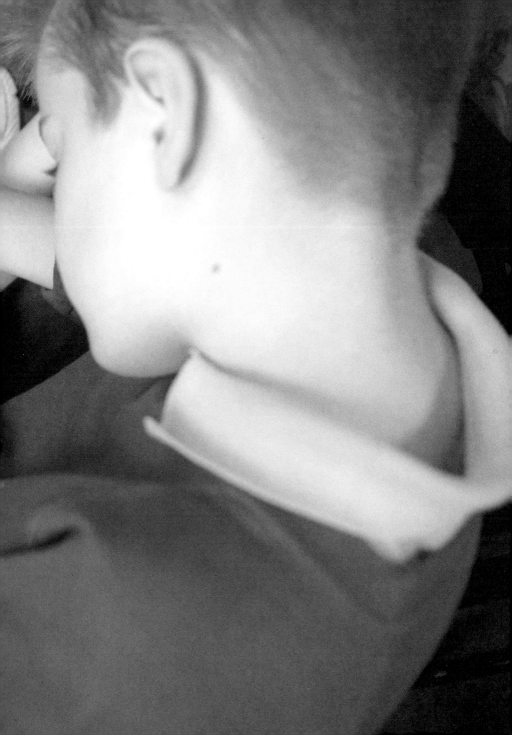

Idle Parenting

Tom Hodgkinson, founder of the *Idler* magazine *(www.idler.co.uk)* might not seem the most obvious person to dish out parenting tips but the father of three (eight, six and four) is a font of wisdom, as his latest book *Idle Parenting* attests. We asked him for his top 10 tips for raising happy, confident kids.

1 'Do less for your child. Small children don't feel wanted or needed in the household, however much they're loved. They get a sense that they are an encumbrance because we do too much for them. When children are not seen as a useful addition to the family labour force they start to get whiny. Get them doing little things like laying the table, washing up, working in the garden. I'm not talking about babies, but children of two or three upwards. When they're small they don't know the difference between work and play. Take advantage of this: children love hoovering. They're very good at getting the dust out of corners.'

2. 'Hang on to your previous life. Going from enjoying a glass of wine with intellectual company to being home alone with a baby can be killing. Parents need adult company and a home that isn't just a re-fuelling station. Get your friends round. Drink alcohol without feeling guilty.'

3. 'Deal with exhaustion by napping whenever you can.'

4. 'Remodel your work life. Work from home, work part-time, start a business. Being a two-full-time-jobs family is dif-ficult. I thought I was doing my bit by earning money, only to come home and be told, "it's alright for you with your pub lunches!"'

5. 'Play more. What used to be called playschool is now called pre-school, to prepare them for the horror of school. The government idea of full-time day care isn't friendly to the family. Be creative. Reject health and safety guidelines. Learning and play should be indistinguishable. Remember that a two year old learns a whole language without a single lesson. With my children it has been fun to do a bit of Latin at home. Arthur can now say "the dog is in the car". Read them poetry and fantastic stories without morals. Play in fields and forests. Make music and merriment.'

6. 'Be thrifty. We put too much work into raising children and spend too much money. Days at theme parks, Nintendo Wiis, all this costs. You don't need to organise every minute of your child's life. Most fathers I know regret not spending more time with their young families. They're away from home making money to spend it on having fun. But you can have lots of fun at home doing nothing and spend-

ing nothing. Schedule a do-nothing day. Don't even plan activities. Children make up their own games. Fantasy-play is very important and they can do that with a cardboard box and a twig. It teaches them self-reliance. Robert Louis Stevenson would play ships in his porridge. We forget, as adults, how imaginative children are.'

7. 'Buy fewer toys. Some people will feel guilty for being away all week and buy a £300 toy to make up for it. Just spend more time at home. That's all they want. We have regular wrestling sessions when all three children jump on me. They love it and it doesn't cost a penny. When our youngest took the card out of the Sky box and lost it, we got rid of the television. They don't miss it at all and you cut down on the advertising that enters your house.'

8. 'Don't spoil them. Be more as well as less strict. There's no need for a choice of juices or breakfast cereals. The purpose of consumerism is to make us feel anxious and inadequate. We deprive our children as much as possible; last Christmas I bought one of them a wooden bagatelle board instead of a Wii. Mind you, it doesn't get much use.'

9. 'Leave the child alone. But not to the extent that it eats nails and pokes its fingers in sockets. We would lie in bed all Saturday morning and soon enough they started getting their own breakfast. This was achieved literally by lying in bed. They even enjoy making us cups of tea because they feel that they are contributing to the house.'

10. 'Embrace responsibility.'

Interview by Robin Barton

gather

SHOPPING WITH SOUL

nurture

play

motion

travel

small

gather

66 **WHAT VALUE DOES AN OBJECT HAVE WHEN YOU CAN BUY 10 MORE EXACTLY THE SAME IN AN INSTANT?** **99**

Bernadette Murphy, *Zen and the Art of Knitting*

Commerce makes the world go around, which is handy to remember if you ever feel guilty about embellishing your life with little luxuries. Shopping fuels the all-important economy, can help raise spirits and be sociable and fun if approached in the right way (which isn't being corralled into sterile superstores and sold mass-produced dross by surly, uninterested staff. Maaaah!).

Many small businesses and traditional shops have disappeared because of our appetite for global trends and compulsion for 'convenience'. The more it happens, the higher price we pay culturally, collectively and individually. Bucking the trend by buying from independent stores and seeking out places with soul helps stimulate creativity, puts money back into the community and takes much of the 'con' out of consuming. It's also a nice change being more than the digits on your credit card.

Shopping

Isn't it ludicrous that 'shopping' – the extravagance of buying stuff we probably don't necessarily need – sometimes feels like a chore? Try shopping the old-fashioned way: bring a friend and make an occasion of it; plan a relaxed pit stop on the way; linger over something that has been handmade; talk to the person who made it (or is at least passionate about what they're selling). Only buy things you love and think of the LATTE factor, favouring stuff that's local, authentic, traceable, trusted and ethical.

RECORDS No one has suffered more from the rise of technology than record shops. But since 1976, when it opened in Talbot Rd, Notting Hill, **Rough Trade** *(www.roughtrade.com)* has actually been gaining ground, slowly edging its way eastward via Covent Garden, and most recently peddling its vibes from the Old Truman Brewery off Brick Lane. It has inoculated itself against the download virus by being passionate about what it peddles, engaging staff for recommendations, and substituting iPod functionality with a human touch.

Vinyl is everything a download isn't: a sensory experience, with a smell as you prise the record from its sleeve, the glossy black sheen and the rich sound with the crackle and pops of the grooves. Soho's Berwick St was traditionally the home of independent shops, but after some high-profile closures few remain. Duncan Kerr's second-hand store, **Revival Records** *(30 Berwick St; 020 7437 4271; www.revivalrecords.uk.com)* bucks the trend and still buys and sells CDs and vinyl.

Hanway St's **On The Beat** *(020 7637 8934)* is doing just fine according to owner Tim. 'Just as there are always people collecting books, there will always be people that collect vinyl. I'm not doing new releases, and if I was I'd probably be in trouble! CDs have got a

lot better since they came out because they're taking their time making them now, but not back in the day. Vinyl's got a warmer sound, especially the old recordings.' Collectors get lost for hours in his cluttered jungle of everything from post-war pop to 1960s beat and rare hip-hop. The only thing he doesn't have much of is classical – but for that, of course, there's **Harold Moore's** *(2 Great Marlborough St; 020 7437 1576)*, one of the most dignified record shops on the planet. It almost didn't survive the rent hikes until a regular customer, 'a nice Brummie engineer', offered to buy the shop and keep it going.

INSTRUMENTS Denmark St is where rock stars from Hendrix to Elton John recorded tracks and bought their instruments. It all started a century ago, when the area's cheap rents attracted musicians and struggling artists. But unlike most iconic streets in central London, where soaring rents push characteristic traders away, Denmark St is still the place to pick up a quality guitar or some rare sheet music.

At **Vintage and Rare Guitars** *(6 Denmark St; 020 7240 7500; www.vintageandrareguitars.com)* you can find 1960s Fender Strats and 1970s Gibsons costing anything from £500 to £3500. Stepping off street level,

Dave King (3rd floor, 21 Denmark St; 020 7836 0816) has been building guitars for more than 20 years. A true perfectionist, each instrument takes him something like 170 hours to craft.

If it's a more unusual sound you're after, you'll find it at the **Duke of Uke** *(22 Hanbury St; www.dukeofuke.co.uk)*. The east London icon is the city's only ukulele and banjo emporium (they can teach you how to play the thing too). They also stock a good range of guitars, mandolins, harmonicas and the like, and organise brilliant little gigs and salons at beautiful and obscure venues across town.

The instruments at **Ray Man** *(54 Chalk Farm Rd; www.raymaneasternmusic.co.uk)* have been gathered from all over the world, and are mostly handmade one-offs. Far from exclusive, staff here actually encourage you to pluck the odd sitar or tap a drum (even if you do need to ask what most of the exotic instruments actually are). It's also a great place to pick up that unusual Tibetan CD or dip into a workshop in Chinese traditional music. The eponymous founder curates the lot; he's a musician, teacher, local legend and an enlightened soul, reportedly uninterested in possessions (well, apart from mandolins and bells and records...), and might just represent the very best of Camden.

BOOKS For a city so rich in literary culture, there are depressingly few local, independent bookstores. The ones that remain listen to customers, offer personality and service, and deserve support. At the risk of offending by omission the bookshops we love dearly, we can't *not* mention a few standout stores. A storybook example, **Village Books** *(1d Calton Ave; 020 8693 2808)* is a cornerstone of the Dulwich Village community. Owners Julian and Hazel are impossibly well-read and only too happy to track down whatever you're after – on that rare occasion they don't have it tucked away on a shelf somewhere – and are so familiar with regulars' tastes that they'll always get recommendations just right.

Resembling a manor house library, the elegantly Edwardian **Daunt Books** at 83 Marylebone High St *(020 7224 2295; www. dauntbooks.co.uk)* might be the capital's most beautiful bookshop, its grand oak shelves stacked with travel tales, biographies and lost classics. Cookery, gardening and fiction occupy the front but the shop's heart belongs to galleries, while stout English names like Chatwin and Newby rub shoulders with wanderlust-inspiring Heinrich Harrer and Antoine de Saint-Exupéry.

The traditional, independent spirit prospers at many second-hand stores (a triumph of soul, environmentalism or tight-fisted-ness?). They seem to survive in even the most unlikely locations, like **Copperfield's**, nestled somewhere between Waterstone's and the Odeon complex in Wimbledon *(37 Hartfied Rd; 020 8542 0113)*. The shop is an Alice-like rabbit hole, where owners Joe and Jane stack books in every dusty cranny: kids' classics under the staircase, old aeroplane manuals on the first floor, wildlife books out the back. A happy hum drowns out the traffic rattling by outside and it's not unusual to see cross-legged readers gorging on Keats in the corner.

Meanwhile, **John Sandoe Books** *(10 Blacklands Tce; 020 7589 9473)* embodies all the class of Chelsea without the Kings Rd commercialism. Across three floors of a

Slow Reading

We suggest that every slow-inclined reader should acquire *In Praise of Slow* and *Under Pressure* by Carl Honoré, which explore our tendencies towards speed and hyper-parenting respectively. We also love Tom Hodgkinson's *How to be Idle*, a collection of witty and informed essays charting a day in the life of an idler, with its joys and perils. The editor of *The Idler* magazine is also the author of *How to Be Free* and *The Idle Parent*. A forefather is Jerome K. Jerome's *Three Men in a Boat* (1889), the account of a boat trip on the Thames taken from Kingston to Oxford by three men and a fictional dog.

beautiful 18th-century building, new and old are stacked side by side, so you're as likely to walk out with the latest *McSweeney's* as you are with a battered old copy of Norman Collins' *London Belongs to Me*. There is a system to the labyrinthine shelves, we're told, but don't expect to crack it in one visit.

Central London has been stained with old ink and critical thought since early last century, when the radical-thinking Bloomsbury Group would meet at 46 Gordon Square. **Persephone Books** *(59 Lamb's Conduit St; 020 7242 9292)* retains the atmosphere, reprinting 'neglected' books by female writers in uniform covers, for a tenner each.

We're also fond of the **London Review Bookshop** *(4 Bury Pl; www.lrbshop.co.uk)*, one of the city's most inspiring independent shops. With its connections to the lofty *London Review of Books*, it's no surprise that staff are so knowledgable; nothing beats an afternoon browsing the shelves and digesting it all over a hearty slice of cake in the cafe.

In nearby Charing Cross Rd, many favourites are struggling to contend with Chinese takeaways and cheap pubs. Most, like the recently-spruced-up-but-still-delightfully-shabby **Quinto** *(48A Charing Cross Rd; 020 7379 7669)*, are trying to balance their traditional higgledy-piggledy charm with the modern-day market. For all their efforts, there's still something amusing about seeing a rare edition of William Blake, worth hundreds of pounds, sharing a shelf with a dusty old one-pound paperback. Nearby **Foyles** *(113–119 Charing Cross Rd; 020 7437 5660; www.foyles.co.uk)* brings together everything we love about the best bookshops – quality, service, intrigue – with five floors of new and old that invite you to lose yourself for hours.

DRINK In contrast to some other independent traders, many traditional alcohol shops are still going strong. If you've ever wondered what Lord Byron weighed, you can find out at **Berry Bros. & Rudd** *(3 St James's St; 0870 900 4300; www.bbr.com)*, the wine merchants that have occupied the corner of Pall Mall since 1765 (when they sold coffee, hence the sign of a grinder outside). Even if you have no intention of splashing £3000 on a bottle of Chateau Pétrus, venture in to see the Finest Reserves room, the lopsided floorboards and the coffee scales on which London's movers and shakers were weighed. And Byron, in case you're wondering, weighed 13st 12lbs at age 18.

For something stronger, **Gerry's Spirits Shop** *(74 Old Compton St; 020 7734 2053; www.gerrys.uk.com)* is one of the last vestiges of Soho's dissipated days, when Jeffrey Bernard propped up the bar in the Coach and Horses and the red light district was in full swing. Here you can get obscure and downright dangerous spirits, and it seems Gerry's should survive as long as there's a market for Choya ginseng liqueur.

SPECIALISTS Against the floral chaos of Columbia Rd Flower Market you'll find **Angela Flanders** *(96 Columbia Rd, Shoreditch; www.angelaflanders-perfumer.com)*, a proper old-fashioned perfumer who is every bit as enchanting as you'd expect from the Victorian appearance of her shop. She has been using natural ingredients to create seasonal perfumes and skincare 'since the spring of 1985', drawing inspiration from her imagination, her emotions, even stories and legends.

We also like her attitude to working hours – the shop is only open on Sundays, when the flower market is in full bloom.

'If you love art, folly or the bright eyes of children, speed to Pollock's,' wrote Robert Louis Stevenson. The toy master himself passed away in 1937 but his magic lives on in **Benjamin Pollock's Toyshop** (*44 The Market; www.pollocks-coventgarden.co.uk*), which sells toy theatres as well as traditional and handcrafted toys, games and classic children's books. This shop might be the loveliest thing about Covent Garden.

At **The Button Queen** (*76 Marylebone Lane; 0207 935 1505*), button monarchs Martyn and Isabel Frith will generally do the rummaging for you – there's simply too much to go through at London's only shop dedicated to buttons. It's more like a museum really, with ceiling-high shelves packed with specimens of every shape and colour, from 19th century picture buttons to the art deco plastic kind, vintage blazer buttons and more modern half-balls and double-flats and acorns (who knew there were so many types?).

Once you've honed your appreciation for the little things from independent traders, indulge yourself at a market. From East End bargains to west London collectibles, gourmet Borough to local neighbourhood staples (p204), there's infinite pleasure to be found fossicking. Nowhere wraps up the quintessential London scene like **antiques markets**, with places like Bermondsey, Greenwich, Portobello Road and Camden Passage flying the flag for tourists and locals alike. Typically, lower rates and higher custom allow independent specialists to survive in markets and arcades.

In the relentless capital, however, nothing's certain, and there's been a somewhat mournful air since The Mall in Islington closed down in 2008. Iconic antique traders were evicted to make way for higher rent-payers. Fearing similar fates, markets and arcades of all persuasions have been scrambling for ideas. One of the most inspired has been the community-minded **'Brixton Pound'**, which has come up with its own local currency to keep money in Brixton.

Old-timers

Among the row of shops on Brushfield St is a little corner of Olde Englande, **A Gold** (*42 Brushfield St; 020 7247 2487*), where you can buy honey mead, Scotch eggs and sugar mice sold in paper bags. As well as making the best sandwiches around Spitalfields, this is a super place to fill up a hamper for a picnic with chutneys, cheeses and lashings of ginger beer. The antique interior is just as delightful to the senses.

Whether it's the fizz of a sherbet lemon or the tartness of a pear drop, whatever taste takes you back to childhood can be found at **Mrs Kibble's Olde Sweet Shoppe** (*57 Brewer St and 4 St. Christopher's Pl; 07961 130503*). Her best-selling sweets are rhubarb and custards – 'though,' she says, 'it all depends what era you were born'.

FASHION London's best tailors won't be hurried, and the words 'Savile Row' are synonymous with slow, from the traditional (Huntsman) to the contemporary (Richard James). **Gieves and Hawkes** *(1 Savile Row)* take up to 40 measurements and 60 hours to create your 'piccolo and flute'. Off this famous strip, **Timothy Everest** *(24 Corbet Pl; 020 7426 4881; www.timothyeverest.co.uk)* settled in Shoreditch long before it was cool. 'I suppose we're something of a hybrid,' he says, blending the craft of the traditionalists with the verve of the new bespoke movement.

Independent local designers showcase their wares at art markets. **Camden Market** and **Portobello Rd** get a bad wrap these days, but we're actually quite impressed with the balance they've found between happily hippie and healthily hip. Even better is the **Sunday UpMarket** in the Old Truman Brewery, a platform for upcoming artists and designers, who are usually the ones manning the stalls.

The mostly-independent boutiques around Spitalfields are, for many artists, a step between having their own stall and their own shop. Despite a recent makeover and the inevitable arrival of cafe chains, this is still the hip retail heart of young London. Take **Tatty Devine** *(236 Brick Lane; 020 7739 9191; www.tattydevine.com)*: founded by art-school graduates Harriet Vine and Rosie Wolfenden in 1996 as a place to sell their own creations, it's since expanded to become a launching pad for other like-minded young designers. Handmade jewellery and bright and quirky shoes are the mainstay, but the pair have their fingers on the pulse of London's indie craft and fashion scene and you never know what you might find.

DIY Sales of sewing machines tripled in 2008, providing proof that creativity booms in times of economic strife – get yours at www.sewantique.com, the Wimbledon-based shop and sewing machine museum. Two magnificent places for raw materials are **Prick Your Finger** (p201) and **I Knit London** in Waterloo *(106 Lower Marsh; 020 7261 1338; www.iknit.org.uk)* where owners Gerard Allt and Craig Carruthers preside over knitting evenings and describe it as 'a place to get inspired'.

The handmade movement is centred on self-expression and the desire for meaningful over mass-produced. It's logical equivalents are brewing your own beer, baking bread, screen-printing T-shirts, pickling vegetables, printing cards, developing photography, building bikes and so on. Doing anything for and by yourself gives a sense of satisfaction that lasts far longer than the retail buzz.

Rebecca Earley is one of the Londoners behind **'upcycling'**, the art of using discarded materials to create something useful and beautiful, like a dress made from old upholstery. The glamorous recycler has her own label, B.Earley, and also works for the Chelsea College of Art and Design, helping inspire others to create fashion that doesn't cost the earth *(www.everandagain.info)*.

Plenty of designers have cottoned onto the benefits of recycling – oh, how do we pick a favourite? **Traid** *(154 Camden High St; www.traid.org.uk)* is a charity shop with a difference: any donated items that are torn, stained or otherwise headed for landfill are instead reconstructed into one-off fashion pieces. What's more, all profits go to recycling activities, education and international development projects.

CLOSE-KNIT FRIENDS RACHAEL AND LOUISE OF PRICK YOUR FINGER

Yarning for a Fight

Johnny Rotten's threadbare jumper sparked a revolution – in knitting. Oh-so-cool (or perhaps just in need of repair), the woolly threads inspired Rachael Matthews and fellow craft-lover Louise Harries to found the **Cast Off** *(www.castoff.info)* knitting club. It challenges the staid reputation of handicraft, and promotes doing craft in public places. Since 2000, hundreds of women and men of all ages have taken up knitting needles in support. They began with simple aims – a toy for a new baby, a beanie in time for winter – but lately there has even been such excitement as a woolly wedding (the dress, the bouquet, the sandwiches!).

The pair met at Central St Martins College of Art & Design. 'Louise was doing knit and I was doing print; we used to do our knitting in the canteen with our thermos flasks.' Bonding over tea and yarn, they generated a welcome waft of subversion at a stage when big business and modern art were getting cosy. 'It was a strange time,' she says. 'Tate Modern had just opened and the Young British Artists seemed untouchable. And here we were knitting little things, as a reaction against mediocrity.'

It was also a stand against disposable fashion and the erosion of community. 'Every new wave of craft has a layer of radicalism, from the women knitting at the guillotine onwards. Many people feel adrift today and they want to feel like they belong. Knitting addresses issues of branding and the sweatshop culture. People take the piss but there is also affection for it,' Rachael laughs.

Rachael and Louise also opened **Prick Your Finger** *(260 Globe Rd; 020 8981 2560; www.prickyourfinger.com)*. The shop spins its own yarn from the highest quality wool, provides free patterns to download, and holds weekly knitting and crochet classes for beginners and 'improvers'. Their humour infuses everything; at Christmas they sell matchbox-sized knitted baby Jesuses, complete with halos.

Both Rachael and Louise grew up in remote farming communities – Rachael in the Lake District and Louise in Wales – and intended Prick Your Finger to restore a lost link between town and country. 'Spinning our own yarn is such a privilege. But it is ethically rather than economically viable. People come in expecting a ball of wool to cost £1 or £2 but they're £8 or £9 because that's how much it costs to produce, with all the regulations.'

The knitting revival is part of a wider craft renaissance, described by Rob Kalin, the founder of www.etsy.com, as 'conscientious consumption'. **Etsy**, a wonderful online marketplace for all things crafty, enables the independent hand-maker to sell their knitted hats, handmade jewellery, woodcuts, cushions, prints, toys and ornaments. It currently lists more than 200 local shops. Both Rachael and Rob agree that making things is also social: 'People want to be part of a community and they want to create heirlooms,' says Rachael. 'It's a lot to do with recreation. We're remaking knitting as a social, environmentally-aware activity and by doing it together there's nothing to be shy about.' ⚘

REFASHION There's a thriving scene in restored and customised clothing too, all part of London's unique street fashion identity. Cheap, sustainable and lots of fun, charity and vintage shopping reverses the guilt of consuming. Savour the rummage and the quest: take in the chatter and hum of the friendly staff (definitely not on commission), try on something ugly from the 80s for a laugh, and then browse at ease in the hope of uncovering a gem.

Thrifty shoppers, like our friend Julia, have some good tips, such as staking out the **charity shops** in posh areas like Kensington and Chelsea – the sort of places where old Yves Saint Laurent gowns could be cleared from wardrobes because they're *so* last season. Thrift shops offer direct lines into particular places, reflecting their locale.

Julia suggests hitting the monthly **Vintage Fashion Fair** *(www.pa-antiques.co.uk)*, usually at Hammersmith Town Hall. But if you want to beat the professional buyers, you'll have to, for a change, get there quick. Their purchases often end up in places like **This Shop Rocks** *(131 Brick Lane; 020 7739 7667)*, a boutique crammed with good quality vintage gear selected by Tim Sanderson, ranging from tea dresses to frock coats. The tiny shop is at the heart of an area packed with vintage stores.

Around the corner is **Absolute Vintage** *(15 Hanbury St; 020 7247 3883; www.absolutevintage.co.uk)*, an emporium where ancient cowboy boots are stacked next to satin gowns. Men need not feel left out: **Old Hat** in Fulham *(62–66 Fulham High St; 020 7610 6558)* is stuffed with classic suits and gentleman's attire. Thanks to David Saxby's keen eye you get a better cut of cloth here.

For accessories, you won't do better than **Bermondsey Antiques Market** *(Bermondsey Square, Southwark)*. Of course, you're just as likely to take home a pair of Georgian candlesticks as the silver earrings you were looking for, but who's complaining? The market kicks off at 4am every Friday and, again, you'll want to get in early before the Portobello Rd on-sellers snap up the best bargains. Our suggestion: wake up to the cry of stallholders, then follow your stomach to nearby Borough Market before crossing the river and walking in to work.

FREECYCLING Rather than throwing away what you don't want any more, give it to someone who'll appreciate it. Join a local **freecycling** *(www.freecycle.org)* group, send them details of that oven or oboe you want to get rid of, or scour the online notice board for something you need. Most of the time you'll have to collect the item but, as the name suggests, it's all free. There are more than 40 groups across London alone.

For Mike Higgins of Crystal Palace, dabbling in freecycling has yielded a composter and baby bottle steriliser, while he has managed to pass on chairs, sound insulation, an amp and building materials. One deal that failed to come was for a washing machine; you've got to move fast for prime items. Mike's advice: have a friend and a car at your disposal.

At **Acton Market** *(The Mount/King St; www.actonmarket.com)*, the last Saturday of the month is Give or Take Day. Basically, you turn up with something you don't need any more, and take home something you do, for free. Change is that simple.

Your Local Market

It's Saturday morning and a couple of old boys are fishing by the water's edge, stocked up with beer and sandwiches. The market crowds mean they probably won't catch anything today, but they don't seem bothered. The burbling water gives way to the tinny sound of a vendor's radio, a keyboardist busking under the bandstand and the smell of curry coming from a nearby stall. It's the same every weekend.

Magi's knitting beanies while her neighbour sits at a sewing machine taking in a vintage coat for a nice old gentleman. A couple of girls try on fancy hats, admiring themselves in the smudged antique mirror on the opposite table, itself stacked with beautiful and utterly useless old things like chipped wire-framed spectacles and mismatched cufflinks. The food section is small, but it's got all the essentials: fresh-baked sourdough and dusty spuds and bright red vine tomatoes and pickled baby beets. A woman in a purple pashmina chats away to the farmer with the nice smile, blushing when her four year old runs up and bowls her over at the knees ('Mummy, mummy, there's a jumping castle!'). In my pre-caffeine breeze I ponder the way the river runs behind the market stalls, nature and trade together flowing through the heart of the neighbourhood, at ease with the rhythm of the locals. 'You alright, love?' the cheese man laughs as he stirs me from my daft reverie. 'Here, try a bit of this.' His cheddar is creamy and crumbly and I'm picturing it with the homemade chutney Kate gave us last week. He wraps up just enough for lunch.

There's a little queue at the coffee stand, but no one's stressed; local chatter blends with the buzz of beans being ground, and I need the time to decide between varieties anyway. As I wait I picture this same scene all over the city, Saturday mornings at the market. Each tends to reflect the character of the neighbourhood; sleepy and unfussed, packed with families and fishermen and women in fraying layers, Merton Abbey Mills certainly reflects mine.

Community markets are not really about what's on the trestle tables, but who's behind them: truly local artisans – painters and jewellers and bakers, all from the neighbourhood. Tea sellers and gardening stalls are unofficial advice centres as much as they are businesses, sharing tips on stress relief or how to grow marjoram. These community gatherings go back centuries in London, when they fuelled the economies and identities of neighbourhoods across town. Here on the banks of the River Wandle, my market would have been an essential outlet for the nearby farm, and the main spot for locals to gather up the bones of a weekly shop. Now we seem to need reminding to shop locally, but when we do it's rewarding for everybody. This Saturday I can barely get in the door at Charlie's Rock Shop – quite a change from a sleepy midweek browse, and a welcome one for any independent trader, I'm sure.

In such a sprawling city, it's too easy to

travel from work to home to that trendy new bar without ever feeling grounded. From Acton to Archway, markets connect us to the people and atmosphere of the place we call home. I used to live by Brixton Market, which had a different vibe to where I am now, but the very same effect. In the slightly grimy arcades, wild yams and whole fresh fish were stacked next to giant boxes of washing powder and cheap linen. It didn't take long to recognise the locals: some would hang outside All Tone Records as the crackly sound system blasted old reggae 45s; others would read their newspapers and catch up on local gossip as they gorged on organic soul food from mismatched china tea sets at Rosie's Cafe. The chaos was calming.

These days, living on the River Wandle, it's the rushing water that grounds me. At the old mill, once the workshop of William Morris and Arthur Liberty, the waterwheel now powers the local pottery. A mum and daughter take a class, crafting bowls from wet clay, and I'm running my own hands along Stephen Llewellyn's fired and finished versions on the shelf. And then a photo catches my eye, five chicks in a nest – 'Grey wagtails,' I'm told upon asking. 'Oh come, I'll show you where their nest was!' Like a proud mum, the shopkeeper takes me inside the waterwheel and points out a little hollow nook in the pillar. 'We turned the mill off for about three weeks so the mum and dad could come in and out easily with the food. I do hope they've survived.' One certainly has, I tell her excitedly; you'll see her just down the river, on the cluster of stones past the next bridge. For weeks the flash of her yellow belly has been brightening up my walk to the Tube. I decide to walk that way now, to see if she's around. Alas, like the fish, she's keeping her distance today. But like the fishermen, I'm not really fussed. I take my cheese and meander home. ☙

Hayley Cull

WE WANTED TO USE THIS PIC, BUT COULDN'T FIND A SUITABLE SPOT, SO INDULGE US PLEASE

Index

T